NAVIGATING STRESS

A MENTAL HEALTH HANDBOOK

TRIGGER™
The mental health & wellbeing publisher

ABOUT THE AUTHOR

Joy Langley has worked for 15 years in the UK as an accredited BACP psychotherapist. She uses cognitive behavioural techniques (CBT) to support clients with issues around stress, anxiety, depression and overwhelm.

She offers online courses and face-to-face workshops, using recognised psychological tools and strategies to help you understand what triggers your stress and how to manage it.

She has worked with MIND for over five years, working with adults suffering from long-term mental health distress.

For more information, worksheets, templates and checklists, please visit:

www.joylangley.com/books/navigating_stress
www.stopfeelingstressedout.com/books/navigating_stress
facebook.com/groups/stopfeelingstressedout.community
www.linkedin.com/in/karenjoylangley

OTHER BOOKS IN THIS SERIES

NAVIGATING STRESS

A MENTAL HEALTH HANDBOOK

HOW TO FIND CALM DURING STRESSFUL TIMES

Joy Langley

Edited by Wendy Hobson

TRIGGER™
The mental health & wellbeing publisher

This edition published in 2023 by Trigger Publishing
An imprint of Shaw Callaghan Ltd

UK Office
The Stanley Building
7 Pancras Square
Kings Cross
London N1C 4AG

US Office
On Point Executive Center, Inc
3030 N Rocky Point Drive W
Suite 150
Tampa, FL 33607
www.triggerhub.org

A CIP catalogue record for this book is available upon request from the British Library
ISBN: 978-1-83796-284-6
Ebook ISBN: 978-1-83796-285-3

Typeset by Lapiz Digital Services

To the synchronicity in the grand universe that took my only (larger than life!) 23-year-old son Riaz Jaye Kamat from this earthly plane because of bipolar, so I could evolve into the person I am today – passionate about suicide prevention, mental 'wealth' for men, and finding ways to protect the human spirit.

CONTENTS

CONTENTS

INTRODUCTION

Have you picked up this book because you are feeling
overwhelmed? Maybe you are worried about feelings of
exhaustion, demotivation and anxiety; perhaps you feel
you are experiencing burnout or simply that uncomfortable
physical and emotional sensations are starting to scare you.
It is most likely that you are under stress.

We all experience stress – even the best life can be
stressful. We usually associate the word with negative
experiences. An intimidating boss or co-worker, petty
arguments with family, unpaid bills piling up, political changes
that affect your community, feuds with neighbours, job
redundancies and more – all these are external stressors on
our lives. But we also have internal stressors: illness, anxious
negative thinking and overwhelmingly powerful emotions such
as fear, anxiety, anger, worry, doubt and panic.

If your ultimate goal is to understand, reduce and manage
stress, you have come to the right place, because that's what
this book is going to help you to achieve. If you are hoping
to find a magic Zero Stress Pill in these pages, I am afraid
you need to go to the fairy tale section because you might
find it there with the unicorns and fairies. But if you come
with an open mind and the mindset that you can reassess

your attitude to stress and how you deal with it, then read on because I can help.

The raw truth is that it is impossible to have a stress-free life – and, in fact, that wouldn't be altogether a good thing, as I will explain. Our body's stress response is instinctive and, you may be surprised to hear me say, a pretty smart biological mechanism. It is part of what is commonly known as our fight-or-flight mechanism, assessing threatening situations and taking appropriate action to protect us.

At best, stress is a motivator that helps us get things done, achieve our goals, know when to ask for support, and help us avoid overburdening ourselves. At worst, it goes into overdrive and makes us so conscious of all the stressors in our lives that we become unable to cope with them.

What I aim to do is to help you recognize the stress triggers that are personal to you, and track the physical, psychological and behavioural reactions you experience as a result of those triggers. Being able to track your unique stressors allows you to achieve a number of benefits. If you work through the text and exercises in this book you should be able to:

- identify the unique stressors in your life, both external and internal
- learn how you react to those stressors, physically, mentally and behaviourally
- understand how to lessen those triggers to avoid hitting your stress tolerance level
- implement strategies to deal with your stress symptoms when they occur.

Using the practical strategies in this book, you can formulate a healthier, fresher mindset that will allow you to cope more confidently with everyday problems.

Stress Is Not the Enemy

You might have heard expressions such as 'stress can kill you', and perhaps you believe it to be true. But viewing stress in this way is not helpful. Stress is a natural and essential part of life. Sorry, it's not going away any time soon. In fact, stress has great value. It is being 'over-stressed' that is the problem.

As with anything in life, you can have too much of a good thing. One doughnut is a real treat; a sack of doughnuts would make us ill. It's just the same with stress.

What we need to do is radically rethink how we deal with stress and find a more responsible perspective. We need to 'make friends' with our natural biological response, get to know it and learn to manage it so that we stop viewing stress as the enemy within and start to befriend it and respect it. We need to understand its good points and learn to manage the bad so that stress is no longer in control – we take back control in order to instil a sense of calm confidence that we shall build greater resilience, tolerance and coping skills.

17.9 million working days were lost in the UK due to stress, anxiety or depression in 2019. That is 51% of work-related ill health cases and 55% of working days lost to ill health (HSE 2019/20).[1]

What Is the Stress Response?

At the heart of understanding stress is knowing what it is, why it is important and how it works. Stress is perfectly normal. We all experience both good and bad things in our lives; the stress response is simply the body's instinctive way of identifying what might genuinely be life threatening.

Humans are designed for survival and the stress alarm acts like a slap in the face! It's an automatic internal system that has evolved to grab our attention, then give us sufficient energy to defend ourselves or flee. For our ancestors, a couple of million years ago, the trigger would have been a life-threatening danger, which is why the stress response is called fight or flight. The body constantly scans the world around us for potentially life-threatening situations, which trip the stress response and give us a boost of energy to help us escape from danger. Although our way of life is now more sophisticated, it takes a long time for evolution to catch up, so we need to adapt our rational response to our automatic stress reaction.

Things that trip our stress reaction now may be physical – from crossing a difficult road junction or moving house to falling sick. Or they may be psychological – feelings of concern, anxiety, worry, doubt and too much predictive thinking can all trigger this sensitive internal alarm.

Accepting Stress as Natural and Necessary

The stress response has been around for millions of years and will never go away; we need it. But we also need to change the way we perceive it so we acknowledge its purpose in identifying threats but accept the responsibility of managing those threats in a positive way. Then we can channel that stress energy to help us accept and rise to life's challenges, viewing them as opportunities to help us learn and grow.

I am grateful for my in-built warning system, although a tad annoyed by its emotional sensitivity. But the good news is that, with a bit of practice, we can all override it's knee-jerk assessment of events and get a speedy second opinion from our rational brain. Only then do we have the power to challenge the original evidence and make a more informed decision on what to do. Understanding the quirkiness of our mind, knowing that it filters information in irrational ways, that it doesn't always differentiate between real or imagined events, and that it communicates its fears automatically to the body's nervous system are worth remembering.

How Come Other People Can Handle Negative Stress?

Everyone responds differently to the multi-layered pressures of life – some more calmly than others – and none of us responds consistently – we may cope with the same situation better on one occasion than another. That is shaped by our genes and also by our life experiences, especially the way we were parented, and the intensity of any traumatic situations faced during early childhood. These experiences can provide some explanation about our current levels of sensitivity, resilience and tolerance to pressure.

There is no point beating yourself up because you feel other people handle stress better than you. Comparisons will not change our experience of a situation; they can only make us feel worse. That is just a waste of precious energy. Acknowledging our vulnerability and learning when to seek help is a sign of strength not weakness.

The best thing we can do is to accept how we feel and stop comparing our feelings to anyone else's. This will prevent feelings of shame and blame and help us move on to the more useful problem-solving strategies.

The Conscious Mind Is the Tip of the Iceberg

Our conscious mind allows us to think, feel and act in any given circumstance. It is like the tip of an iceberg that floats above the surface of the water.

Below the waterline is the other 90% of our mind: our unconscious. That stores all the rules we've put in place about how we should think, feel or behave in situations, what we feel about other people and how we see the world. The unconscious mind works on autopilot, steered by old experiences. The reason this is important is that our subconscious programming can be hard to break, so we should not to be too hard on ourselves while we take the time needed to reprogramme our subconscious. You can do this by activating a process called neuroplasticity, which simply means that the brain is capable of change.

Changing Your Brainwaves

Neuroscientists have demonstrated that the brain can change and adapt as a result of new experiences. This process of neuroplasticity allows the brain's neurons to fire and rewire, creating new memories, ways of thinking and behaviours.

As we encounter hurdles and obstacles, we become increasingly skilled at surmounting them, even when situations feel permanent and impossible to solve. Like a small blot of blue ink dropped into a cup of water, difficulties can feel pervasive and personal; gradually we persuade ourselves that this could only happen to us, exacerbating our stress response.

According to the *New York Post* in 2019, about half of Americans looked on the positive – they were glass-half-full people – while the rest were glass-half-empty or undecided.[2] That still suggests that half the population is focusing on the negative. This negativity bias is like wearing dark glasses all the time, giving us the impression that our surroundings are dark and gloomy, when that may not be the case.

We can discard those negative glasses and see the world for what it is: some good, some bad, but everything ripe for improvement.

A Note About Your Mental Health

How do you know you are having a heart attack, an allergic reaction or have a broken bone? There are obvious signs and painful symptoms that tell you something out of the ordinary is happening. Psychological and emotional distress are less obvious to spot.

Poor mental health can build up gradually in response to the daily hassles of life, or it can happen due to one traumatic event. Left unchecked, stress can become chronic and a problem that increases in severity. It is therefore important that you are alert to symptoms of poor mental health and ask for professional support straight away.

There is nothing to feel ashamed about if you are experiencing mental illness. If you or someone else is worried about any symptoms you are experiencing, please consult a doctor or a mental health practitioner without delay and they can signpost you to local services. If you are experiencing thoughts of self-harm or suicide, seek immediate help from your doctor or an emergency helpline.

If you can hang on to that stress energy but redirect it in a
positive way, then it will not be wasted.

Reprogramming Your Stress Response:
How This Books Works

In this book, I am going to give you a toolkit to help you
successfully handle stress. We will consider:

- **What makes you stressed?** Some people worry about
  being punctual, for example, others don't. Learn to identify
  what stresses you out, physically and mentally.
- **What happens to you when you are stressed?** Do you
  experience physical symptoms like headaches or stomach
  pains? Is your response to feel anxious? Or do you pace
  about or exhibit other behavioural symptoms?
- **How can you modify your reaction to stress triggers**?
  Learn to view your triggers calmly to take away their power
  over you.
- **How do you deal with the symptoms of stress?**
  Even when you are stressed, you can turn that to your
  advantage.

Energy is just power – in itself, it is not good or bad. We need
to learn how to put our stress energy to good use: to help us
pass an exam, deliver a knock-out presentation at work, ace a
job interview or make a great wedding speech.

It is possible to turn negative energy to positive if we take back control.

Documenting Your Learning

Throughout the book, you will gather techniques that help you self-soothe and calm down; they will help you make useful predictions about the enormity of a threat, and enlighten you as to when to seek extra resources when needed.

Start a journal or notebook to keep all your notes as you work through this programme. Most people like a paper notebook, but you can keep notes on your phone, your voice recorder or computer. Note the date every time you make an entry so you can track your progress. It doesn't have to be just a written record. Feel free to do some doodling or creative artwork if that helps you capture the spirit of what's happening to you. Don't wait for me to remind you to use your notebook; add things to it when they are fresh in your mind or that you feel are important.

You will be doing a series of exercises to test and expand your knowledge of your stress and how to bring it under control. So grab a notepad and pen dedicated to gathering information on your stress response.

Tracking your Stress Levels

For any improvement to be quantifiable, you need a baseline reading. Before I start to introduce you to your own stress and how to take control of it, we will begin by assessing and recording your baseline Stress Energy Assessment (SEA) through two assessment tools (which we will come to below).

At the end of each chapter I will prompt you to update your SEA so you will gradually, step by step, see your stress levels decrease. You will hopefully see a quantifiable improvement as you navigate your way through the stress in your life until you find a better place.

EXERCISE: Keep an Open Mind

Changing how you think about stress can actually make you healthier. In this exercise, you will reframe any fear-based ideas that all stress 'can kill'.

- Open a new page of your notebook and write the heading: 'Stress is a natural part of life'. Notice your internal self-talk. Did you think 'no' or 'yes'?
- Read over the introduction and make sure you understand the purpose of the stress response mechanism and why it is important.
- Look back at recent events. Write down three to four situations when your stress response has been triggered by a real threat. Then write down the same number of times when the stress response has been triggered, you wobbled, but continued with the task in hand (it was positive). You may want to include things

you worried about happening, where the event took
place in your mind (this is called rumination).

- Use your imagination. For each event, write down the
value or lack of value in having the stress response
kick in (the consequence).
- Remind yourself to be open to change (we are no
longer hunters living in caves, after all!). Remember,
human beings are good at adapting. Before we
had a lightbulb we thought candles were pretty
illuminating; before we had cars, the horse and cart
was the smartest way to get from A to B. How many
instances of progress can you think of that make
you feel glad that things can change?

Keep your mind open to possibilities. It may take
time and practice to achieve. But when you start to
see that doors can close but others open at the same
time, the sooner you will begin to take control of
your future.

Your Stress Energy Assessment

We are going to start with your first SEA reading and assess
how stressed you are feeling right now.

There is no definitive, scientific questionnaire to assess
the common symptoms of negative stress, although research
scientists Holmes and Rahe created a stress scale in 1967
(see page 81). There is also a diagnostic tool called the patient

health questionnaire (PHQ9 and GAD7) developed by Pfizer and research partners to assess depression and anxiety.[3]

I am going to use a simple set of 10 symptoms, based on ideas from this diagnostic tool, for you to self-assess on a scale of 1–10, plus a single overall baseline figure.

You can either take the two baseline assessments weekly over a period of 4–6 weeks, or as you complete each chapter of the book (depending on how quickly you read them), or monthly.

As you repeat the assessments, and gradually build up coping mechanisms and knowledge, you should see a gradual reduction in your stress levels. By the end of the book, the comparison of your final ratings with your baseline assessment should demonstrate just how far you have travelled towards a calmer, confident and more fulfilling life.

What Do I Mean by 'Stress Levels'?

Judging where you fall on a scale of 1–10 is never easy, but you need to make a judgement call for your baseline assessment. This will be your reference point whenever you need to compare future ratings. Over time, the ratings provide clear evidence that you are feeling better or worse, and by how much. With this in mind, it's a good idea to write yourself some brief notes to remind yourself how you were feeling at the time you did the assessment.

EXERCISE: Baseline Stress Energy Assessment

This exercise will define your current stress level (how much you feel under pressure) so you can use it as a comparison to rate your improvement.

Either focus on your general stress level or choose one to three critical life events bothering you right now and record them separately. For example, you might list moving house, marital problems, examinations, financial difficulties or issues over children's schooling. Keep to a maximum of three otherwise you will lose focus.

For each one, rate how stressed you feel because of that situation on a scale of 1–10, where 1 = not at all stressed, 5 = stress is beginning to have a negative impact on your life and 10 = you feel as though stress is taking over your life.

Issue 1: ....

My current rating is .... Date ....

Issue 2: ....

My current rating is .... Date ....

Issue 3: ....

My current rating is .... Date ....

EXERCISE: Lifestyle Self Assessment

Please answer yes or no to these 10 questions.

1 Has your concentration and ability to judge situations deteriorated?   yes   no

2 Do you worry about your ability to get things right?   yes   no

3 Do you feel overwhelmed or confused by the tasks you have to do?   yes   no

4 Do you have trouble falling asleep or staying asleep?   yes   no

5 Has your appetite changed (overeating or undereating)?   yes   no

6 Have you noticed your energy level is low or you feel exhausted?   yes   no

7 Do you get headaches, aches and pains or stomach problems?   yes   no

8 Are you easily irritated or angry with people for no reason?   yes   no

9 Are you more dependent on nicotine, alcohol, caffeine or non-medicated drugs?   yes   no

10 Are you unable to relax and have fun (and keep thinking about work or family issues)?   yes   no

Number of yes answers ....

Date ....

Make a note of your scores and add a sentence or two about what was is troubling you and why you think it has made you feel anxious. This will enable you to track your progress toward a calmer, confident and happier life.

If you have thoughts of self-harm or suicidal thoughts, please seek professional help immediately. See page 211 for information on where to seek help.

Plotting your progress

Once you have completed these assessments, create a graph to record your baseline ratings. You will be plotting the progress of your:

- Baseline Stress Level Assessment Score: either the three separate individual issues chosen, or, if you prefer, obtain an average assessment for the three issues chosen by adding the individual issue scores and divide by three
- Lifestyle Self Assessment Score (number of 'yes' answers).

The horizontal axis is your progress over time as you move from week to week; the vertical axis is your stress score (maximum of 10) An example is shown opposite.

Each time you revisit these assessments, add your scores to the graph. Over the coming weeks, you will create an instant visual of your progress.

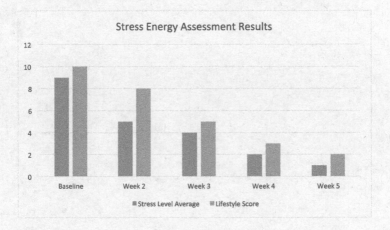

1

WHAT IS STRESS AND WHY DOES IT HAPPEN?

There are many dictionary definitions of stress. Although this one is a bit of a mouthful, it's pretty accurate:

> *'A specific response by the body to a stimulus, as fear or pain, that disturbs or interferes with the normal physiological equilibrium of an organism. Physical, mental, or emotional strain or tension.'*[4]

The term stress has its origins in the Latin word *stringere* (to draw tight), although at that time it was used only to describe hard physical work. We can thank scientific breakthroughs from the 1920s onwards by notable researchers Dr Walter Bradford Cannon, who coined the term 'fight or flight', and Dr Hans Seyle, considered to be the grandfather of stress research, who borrowed the word 'stress' from the field of physics. Dr Seyle went against the grain, challenging the belief that physical reasons were the sole cause of illness. He put forward the revolutionary idea that illness can be caused by stress, 'the non-specific response of the body to change'.

A Three-step Process

Seyle described a three-step stress process called the General Adaptation Syndrome.

- **The alarm stage:** This is triggered by a stressor – this is any physical, emotional or mental situation that kick-starts the fight-or-flight stress response.
- **The resistance stage:** Where the body learns to adapt and cope with difficult events in the short term and return to normal.
- **The exhaustion stage:** This takes over when we are exposed continuously and repetitively to situations we cannot cope with.

Seyle introduced the word 'stressor' to define the causes that trigger the human stress response; we'll examine the different types in chapter 4.

The world still seems happy to measure human suffering in these terms. However, we must stop and give serious thought to whether fear-filled narratives are sensible, kind or just plain irresponsible. There is a heavy emotional and psychological price to pay for maintaining the following three beliefs: stress is inevitable, chronic stress is a killer and our ultimate fate is death by stress exhaustion or burnout.

Modern research continues to examine the elusive dark cloud called stress without paying enough attention to the silver lining. But looking for the positive energy of stress is crucial if we are going to avoid mental health issues across all age groups. While people often cite the mental health problems in store for Generation Z – our teenagers and young people (13- to 23-year-olds)[5] – there are also huge work, time and social pressures on most working adults, children and the retired. Negative stress is a health risk for all age groups.

Stress Triggers – External and Internal Stressors

The word 'stress' has become the go-to-word for any frustrating, annoying, unwanted or scary life event. From breaking a well-manicured nail to being under threat of redundancy, from being devastated your football team lost a match to having to cope with a seriously ill relative. Causes of stress are known as stressors or stress triggers, and they can be internal or external. Whatever triggers your stress the response will be automatic. They can also be positive (good) or negative (bad).

External stressors: These triggers are generally outside our control. They include things such as the environment, the weather, political or social issues, company restructures and downsizing, or the neighbour from hell moving in next door.

Internal stressors: Psychological triggers, on the other hand, are things such as negative thinking habits, negative self-talk, attitudes and expectations, memories and emotional state, mental and physical illness, or undergoing medical procedures. They can be triggered by emotional moments of fear, doubt, worry, concern, anxiety and the powerful 'what if?' question.

So that gives us the start of a list of anomalies to resolve.

- Given the common assumption that stress is always bad and can kill us in the end, how can some stressors be good?
- Why is it that everyone reacts to stressors differently and experiences stress differently?

- And why is it that sometimes we handle an identical situation really well, yet on another occasion we're a bag of nerves?

Let's investigate this a bit further.

Positive and Negative Stress

There are a lot of misconceptions and confusing language surrounding the stress experience, fundamentally because we use 'stress' to mean something that is always negative, when originally it only indicated pressure, which can be good or bad. Bad stress is often called 'distress' and, sadly for us, we are much more familiar with that. Good stress is known as 'eustress', 'eu' being the Greek prefix meaning 'good'.

Negative stress: Very familiar. We have already cited some examples involving relentless negative pressure.

Good or positive stress: This is important for our wellbeing. It is vital for motivation, productivity, performance, accomplishing daily tasks and preventing boredom. It gives us the desire and energy to do the ordinary things, such as get out of bed in the morning, fight our way through rush-hour traffic, meet a deadline at work, visit the dentist. Good stress can also feel exciting, sharpen our focus, increase alertness and help us raise our game, whether we are riding a rollercoaster, taking an exam, watching a horror film or going on a first date.

These are everyday events. Out-of-the-ordinary events can also involve positive stress; they are designed to grab our attention and give our brain that frisson of danger that feels just a bit dangerous. There are so many examples of life events that involve an element of stress but are nonetheless positive: having a baby, getting married, the first day of a new job, going on holiday, moving home.

Many life events involve an element of 'discomfort' but that doesn't mean they are negative, even though recent generations have mistakenly adopted this attitude.

Acute or Episodic Stress and Chronic Stress

Stress varies depending on its duration.

- **Acute stress:** Most stress is acute: it is short in duration so we experience the pressure but bounce back quickly.
- **Episodic stress:** This happens when a stressor occurs regularly, such as always running late in the morning for work or school or getting annoyed at spam emails.
- **Chronic stress:** Experiencing a recurring and intense stressor that you can't get away from.

The physical signs and symptoms are similar for acute and episodic stress: racing heart, high blood pressure, tense muscles, sweating, butterflies in the stomach and more. The same is true of chronic stress, but because we are constantly exposed to the triggers, it is hard to shrug off. Its slow, nagging nature will start affecting our physical, mental and emotional functioning and make us susceptible to disease. At its worst, chronic stress can lead to a debilitating health condition called 'burnout'.

Coping with Stress

Building up a background knowledge of stress – rather than relying on what we think we already know – is crucial before we move on to explaining how you can cope with your stress. As the old saying goes: 'Know your enemy'. You cannot change a habit of thought, emotion or behaviour and start to manage your stress until you identify what contributes to the problem.

Even before we embark on the detail of managing your stress, begin to be alert to the situations, people, activities or places that trigger your stress response. Jot them down in your notebook with dates, times and circumstances in which you experienced them. This will demonstrate the slow build up of stress.

Also record any chronic stress symptoms, such as persistent tiredness, loss of motivation and brain fog, as they can be a big neon sign pointing towards burnout. This will all be useful when we go into more detail in subsequent chapters.

The Reasons the Stress Response Evolved

Two million years ago, our ancestors had very straightforward needs; just food, shelter and warmth. Hunting for food took up a huge proportion of their time and carried the risk of injury or death, so their stress response evolved to help them cope with the dangers of hunting. This stress or threat response transformed the body's physiology and biology into a survival machine: eat or be eaten, stand and fight or flee! The heart pumped faster, blood pressure increased, the liver released glucose ensuring energy to power-up the legs and arms, the body sweated to prevent overheating, the stomach gurgled and churned through being shut down, and they may even have vomited or felt the urge to go to the 'loo'. Does any of this sound familiar?

Evolution is a slow process, to say the least, and we are still subject to the same fight-or-flight response. Modern-day stressors may be less life-threatening than being attacked by a mammoth, but our response to stress triggers hasn't changed much. However uncomfortable it might be, the hormones that are activated by the stress response (of which, more later) give us more energy, physical strength, focus and alertness. We have just replaced wild animals with the regular daily hassles we encounter – a child falling ill, a drop in internet speed, forgetting to pay a bill, delivering a presentation at college or work, our social media 'likes' plummeting.

Five Trauma Responses

The brain is well designed to respond quickly to changes in our emotional state. At the centre of the brain is the limbic system, which could be called our 'emotional fear brain'. All animals have a variation of this as it's critical for survival. When humans feel threatened, the emotional centre overrides the rational brain, ensuring we do whatever's necessary to stay alive until the danger passes. The threat response can be triggered by fear, feeling trapped, abandoned, unsafe, not listened to or supported, invalidated or not acknowledged. Clearly not all of these are life-threatening.

Fight or flight are the first two responses to danger and are well known but, in fact, there are five trauma responses: fight, flight, freeze, flop, fawn.

The freeze response creates temporary body paralysis and we act like a rabbit caught in the headlights. The freeze response can make us feel numb, cold, restrict or hold our breath, or shut down part of our thinking skills so we dissociate and become forgetful. It is another way of the body protecting itself, especially during a traumatic event. The body's nervous system is actually switching from sympathetic (fight-or-flight mode) to parasympathetic (relax mode). To snap out of this we can try shaking our body, like animals do, as a way to release pent-up energy and reset the nervous system.

The fourth trauma response is flop. If freeze doesn't get you out of trouble, the mind and body completely shut down: we collapse or faint, the muscles go floppy and we are compliant.

Finally, there is the stress response known as fawn, which essentially means trying to please, appease or flatter someone by forming a protective bond with the person threatening you (in order to stay alive).

Fight, flight and fawn are active stress responses, freeze and flop are passive. Each response serves and protects us, helping us to survive danger and live to tell the tale.

Tend and Befriend

So, given that not all so-called threats are life-threatening, is there an alternative to fight-or-flight? Yes, 'tend and befriend'.

In 1994, Dr Stephen Porges discussed an evolutionary idea explaining why social engagement instinctively happens when we are faced with threat. The Polyvagal Theory[6] showed the calming role played by oxytocin in response to stress and trauma. The neural pathways in the vagus nerve regulate the autonomic process (automatic body process controlled by nervous system) and encourages positive social behaviour.

During the early 2000s, researchers started investigating this alternative response. Dr Shelley E. Taylor coined the phrase 'tend and befriend' in 2006 as an alternative theoretical response to stress. For example, humans have long pregnancies, produce a limited number of children, and the babies need total care from the start. Children can't run fast enough to escape from predators and are not strong enough to protect themselves from attack; what protects them is the mother's strong maternal instinct, combined with a network of supportive family or friends. This behaviour reduces stress and anxiety among the group and is an evolutionary adaptation for mammals, including humans, across cultures.

In the face of danger, when the threat response is not viable, we reduce stress by caring, nurturing and tending to the weak and vulnerable. Secondly, we gather resources and seek or befriend others, forming protective co-operative bonds.

Biological history means that, in general, women are particularly skilled at forming stable close attachments with other women and seeking the safety of the pack. It appears that the hormone oxytocin is the game changer, as it responds differently to female or male reproductive hormones. Oxytocin is designed to help with reproduction, childbirth, emotional regulation and positive social behaviour. A rise in oxytocin helps us bond, builds trust, increases empathy and aids positive communication, especially when we feel socially isolated or believe we or our close relationships are threatened. The increase in oxytocin is a biological signal that pushes us towards defensive or protective affiliations, the result being a tendency to pull together in a crisis, to bond together, to tend and befriend.

By the same token, the men – the hunters, if you like! – have a tendency to outward expressions of bravery or aggressive reactions. If they can't hunt a mammoth in modern day society – they exercise! But our social structure is a little more complex than it was two million years ago so, while those instincts remain, and physiologically women are more likely to tend and befriend, it is a stress reaction that we can all practise.

Have you ever witnessed someone – male or female – show an incredible act of bravery in order to help someone in danger? We hear many stories about ordinary people doing extraordinarily brave things to help a complete stranger, some even losing their lives in the process. Or perhaps you've witnessed a caregiver going to extreme lengths to protect a child? The ability to transform threat energy into tend-and-befriend energy is all around us.

We can conclude that the physical stress sensations that fill us with energy can be reinterpreted, reframed, repurposed and channelled in a variety of ways. That stress energy can be used positively to deal with threats, build networks, make connections, support and soothe vulnerable members of the tribe. This is a theme that will recur throughout this book because I want you to rethink the way we channel stress energy when it is triggered by situations in our lives.

Giving and Receiving

Just as with any kind of friendship, tend and befriend is a two-way process. Sometimes you are the person receiving the support, and sometimes the one giving the support.

Giving tend and befriend: This might include any of the times we have intervened to remove stressors for someone else, perhaps offering to take a task from a colleague to lighten their load or picked up a friend's children from school when they needed to be in two places at once. It might also cover helping someone to cope with the symptoms of stress, such as running a hot bath for your partner at the end of a long day. On a broader level, you could help to reduce other people's stress by volunteering for a cause you believe in, helping out during natural disasters or offering food or shelter to a stranger. During the COVID-19 pandemic in 2020–21, we witnessed countless heroes emerging from all walks of life to tend and befriend others resulting in a reduction in stress for both parties.

Receiving tend and befriend: You will always remember the gestures – small or large – that helped you get through a stressful time: when a colleague helped you out at a presentation when you got tongue-tied; that brief hug that reassured you that you were not alone; the person who picked you up and took you home when you fell down in the street.

Some people even make tending and befriending their professional career: doctors, nurses, carers, firefighters, police, ambulance staff, first responders and many more.

EXERCISE: Have You Shown the Tend-and-befriend Response?

This exercise is designed to make you look at your own experience of the tend-and-befriend response to prove that stress energy can be a positive force in your life.

- Write in your notebook an incident in which you used the tend-and-befriend response to channel your stress energy. What would have happened if you had used the threat response instead? Which response was better?
- Write about a time you have been on the receiving end of someone re-channelling their stress energy to support you during a difficult situation. It can be anything from a friendly handshake or smile to helping in a dangerous or even life-threatening situation.

In future, when an incident happens that demonstrates the positive use of stress energy, write it in your notebook so you build a library of examples to look back at.

EXERCISE: What's Your Stress Story?

In this chapter we have looked at the evolutionary and physiological explanations of why humans experience stress. Understanding this is crucial, as it stops us feeling like a victim to the ups and downs of life. It's good to write down a simple definition of what stress means to you, and to write your own stress story. In case you have difficulty getting started, take a look at mine.

A chapter in my personal stress story:
Stress impacts my work, especially when I have deadlines or things I don't understand so put off doing (procrastination). Writing this book was stressful! Stress impacts my relationship with my partner and colleagues because I get impatient and annoyed by their demands and the fact they carry out tasks differently to me. My signs are emotional overwhelm, it affects my mental focus, concentration and memory. I also notice the tension in my body, a thumping heartbeat, a gurgling stomach with the urge to go to the toilet. I have the 'freeze' stress response and find it hard to think or move.

Have a go at writing down your own feelings about stress. Remember there are no right or wrong answers – this is about gathering personal information and focusing your thoughts on exactly what stress looks like for you.

Working out your own stress pathways are critical. When you can spot patterns in good times and channel your stress energy, you can return to normal functioning with the minimum of distress.

Stress Energy Assessment

Now you have read this chapter, rerun your Stress Energy Assessments (pages 14–15) applying your new understanding, and fill in your progress graph.

2

HOW STRESS AFFECTS THE BODY
AND THE MIND

In the introduction I asked 10 lifestyle questions to widen your awareness of whether stress is affecting your daily life. The signs and symptoms covered poor concentration; increased worry and irritability; changes to sleep and appetite; increase in smoking, drugs, alcohol and caffeine; lower energy levels and ability to relax; more headaches, aches and pains; and, finally, increased thoughts of self-harm or suicide.[7]

Stress is the internal survival alarm. It switches on to warn us of threats and switches off when the danger is over. The problem is, we are not great at shutting it down. The subconscious mind finds it hard to let go of bad past experiences, and the conscious mind tends to over-think and worry (ruminate) about bad future experiences. This keeps the stress response lurking in the background, similar to a car idling on the driveway. Stress symptoms therefore persist long after challenging events have happened, and can eventually show up as physical illness or emotional and mental distress.

To help us break these cycles, this chapter looks right under the skin – literally! – at how the brain works in relation to stress, how the brain is different from the mind, and how we can take control of both.

The Brain and the Mind

You might be wondering what the difference is between the brain and the mind. Technically they are not the same thing. The brain is a physical vital organ, like the heart, lungs, kidneys and liver. It is protected by the skull, and it processes and stores information. It is also the source of intelligence which we call 'the mind'.

The brain is our control centre, we rely on it to be the conductor of our orchestra, the body. It is arguably the most important organ, as it controls all the other organs and parts of the body, sending and receiving instructions via electrical signals using two smart internal systems. The first is the endocrine system, also known as the hormonal system, and the second is the nervous system, which includes the autonomic stress response system. All of this complex activity happens without input from the conscious mind. You don't have to remember to breathe, to digest your food or worry about missing the next heartbeat. The brain maintains this delicate balance – called homeostasis – across the organs, blood vessels and cells.

The Mind – Conscious and Subconscious

The intelligent mind was always thought to be invisible, but with modern brain scanning techniques we know better, as we can witness sections of the brain lighting up with electrical activity when carrying out a task. The mind never stops thinking, and we've all had many a late night wishing it would keep quiet.

The mind operates at two levels: the conscious and the unconscious or subconscious. It's hard to believe, but the conscious mind controls a mere 5–10% of the mind's capacity. That's the part of us that is aware of the present moment: the part that is reading this book, is aware of who we are and makes decisions about what we do. The remaining 90–95% is controlled by the subconscious and is beyond our awareness. We haven't a clue what information is stored there. It also runs patterns and templates on autopilot based on situations, things we've said, done or felt. It holds onto our assumptions, rules and beliefs.

We use our conscious mind and our five senses to keep track of what's happening outside in the environment, paying particular attention to our safety and survival. We consciously create perceptions, emotions, thoughts, imagination and memories during daily life, then store them away in the subconscious.

A healthy mind stores the positives and negatives, but also learns from new experiences and moves on. A troubled mind has difficulty living in the moment, holds on to stressful events from the past and dwells on and projects frightening thoughts about the future.

The Human Intelligence

The intelligent mind doesn't live in one fixed place; intelligence exists in every nook and cranny of the body, in the tiniest bits of our biology at a cellular level. This intelligence also exists in the heart organ and the gut organ, which are considered to be the second and third brains. From this point onwards I will talk about the brain as the organ and the mind as the conscious thought creator.

The body and mind share the same mission statement – survival! To this end, they constantly communicate data to one another via the smart biological messaging process involving the hormonal system (endocrine system) and the nervous system. They are a great team, and the most valuable assets we will ever possess. It's practically impossible to disconnect the actions of one from the reaction of the other, although some mindful and meditative practices claim to. If we look after both of them, they will help us to achieve our wildest dreams, our biggest ambitions and life goals.

The Brain

Housed inside the skull, this vital organ weighs about 1.5kg (3lb) and is the most complex part of the human body, requiring 20% of the body's blood supply, which delivers vital oxygen and glucose to the brain to allow it to function. The brain controls every vital function from breathing to digestion, heartbeat to swallowing, sleep patterns, memory, cognitive skills and emotion. Conscious thought enables us to solve problems and apply moral, cultural and social codes. The brain can even compensate for deficiencies when other parts of the brain are injured or malfunctioning.

The brain is split into three main parts: the cerebrum, cerebellum and brain stem.

- The cerebrum, or cerebral cortex, is the wrinkly outer part. It is the largest of the three sections and has a right and left hemisphere that control human intelligence – our thinking, learning, speech, reading, co-ordinated movement, creativity, behaviour and interpretation of the outside world using the five senses.
- The cerebellum (Latin for 'little brain') is located underneath the cerebrum and is involved with balance and posture.

- The brain stem connects the cerebrum and cerebellum to the spinal cord and regulates the body's non-conscious vital functions via the central nervous system (CNS), which has over 100 billion nerve cells (neurons) that talk to one another along wire-like structures joined by junctions called synapses.

The Central Nervous System (CNS)

The central nervous system is a huge communication network inside the body comprising of the brain, spinal cord and countless nerves. If we attempted to join up all the nerves in the body it could run for more than 60km. The central nervous system is the control centre and runs through the spinal cord. It uses electrical impulses to receive and despatch data from vital organs, sensory organs (eyes, ears, mouth, nose and skin), and from the network of nerves spread throughout the entire body. The nerves that branch from the spinal cord are known as the peripheral nervous system, or PNS. The nerves that branch from the PNS are the autonomic nervous system (ANS) and control involuntary functions that are essential for survival: heart rate, digestion, respiratory rate, pupil dilation and so on. These nervous systems work without conscious thought from us.

Another way of understanding this is to imagine the CNS that runs through the spinal cord like a motorway or freeway, with the PNS system the town road branches. The PNS has further sub-divisions known as the autonomic nervous system (ANS), which we could call the country lanes.

Along these small country lanes are the nervous systems responsible for the fight-or-flight stress response (the sympathetic nervous system) and for rest and digest (the parasympathetic system).

The nervous system works closely and constantly with the hormonal system to detect and communicate perceived threats, deal with them and reset itself.

The Limbic System (Emotional and Mood Centre)

The limbic system is the part of the brain that takes over when we are stressed. It hijacks our rational cognitive centre, making us overly emotional, irrational, forgetful and lose concentration.

It is located on top of the brain stem and controls subconscious, instinctive emotions and behaviours: the basic need for safety, survival and reproduction; the fight-or-flight response; feeding and caring for our young. It affects our moods and behaviour, and influences bodily functions such as digestion and urination. The limbic system also supports memory storage and retrieval, and monitors glucose, salt, hormones and blood pressure.

The brain's limbic system includes the amygdala, hypothalamus, pituitary gland and the hippocampus, linked on what is called the HPA (hypothalamus-pituitary-amygdala) axis. When we instinctively feel threatened, the amygdala sends out a distress signal to the hypothalamus, which releases adrenalin, giving us a boost of energy. When that boost runs out, a message goes to the pituitary gland, which pumps cortisol into the bloodstream. Both are designed to help us fight or run.

The Reticular Activating System

This is the part of our brain that keeps us alert and awake and it is housed in the brain stem. It plays an important role in filtering data we take in through our senses, and deciding what's important. Have you noticed when you start looking for a specific model of a red car suddenly that's all you notice? That's the RAS doing its job. However, beware, it's also responsible for cognitive biases and distortion: giving us more of what we already know by seeking out information that matches and validates our existing belief.

The Enteric Nervous System (ENS) – The Gut

The word enteric means 'of the small intestine' and this system contains elements of the ANS autonomic nervous system. The gut is often called the third brain, with the heart being cited as the second. The ENS can operate independently of the central nervous system, influencing the digestive process via a network of sensory and motor neurons (nerve cells). It is embedded in the wall of the gastrointestinal tract, which runs from the mouth to the rectum. Hundreds of millions of nerve endings pick up on threats in the environment and can create stress sensations – hence we talk about having a gut feeling.

That gut sensation is transferred to the brain via the spinal nerve and vagus nerve, and the brain translates it into a feeling we can understand: butterflies, a knotted or a gurgling stomach. The uncomfortable sensation is the temporary shutting down of the digestive system. Short-term stress therefore affects appetite and digestion slows down.

The Power of Hormones

We have a 'smart' body – we don't always have to tell it what to do, it manages perfectly well by itself – and stressful events automatically activate the levels of stress hormones adrenalin (also known as epinephrine), norepinephrine and cortisol. The activation of the stress hormones affects many other parts of the hormone (endocrine) system, and the body cleverly works out what else is needed to combat the stress. This includes producing oxytocin to help us bond and connect with others; dopamine, which oversees our challenge and motivation system; serotonin and endorphins, which moderate our mood, wellbeing and happiness; and insulin, which regulates blood sugars (glucose) and provides boosts of energy.

When we are frightened or facing a real or imagined crisis, the adrenal glands release the hormone adrenalin. It is a biochemical messenger that communicates with our brain, preparing us for action. Adrenalin constricts the blood vessels, forcing the heart to pump blood to muscles and quickening the heartbeat. It also increases blood pressure and makes us breathe faster. The biggest benefit of adrenalin? It makes us hyper-alert, hyper-focused, stronger and able to respond more quickly.

During a threat, the brain needs more oxygen and more energy. Adrenalin is effective for approximately 20 minutes, so if the danger is still present, more energy is needed. Cue the pituitary gland in the brain, which tells the adrenal glands to release cortisol. Cortisol releases proteins and fat from our fat stores to provide extra glucose for energy. But the biggest benefit of cortisol? It helps us stay hyper-alert for a few hours, it helps clot the blood and is a powerful opioid painkiller (similar to morphine), so if we are injured in action we can ignore the pain until the immediate danger has passed.

The hormonal cocktail delivers the right amount to deal with full-scale threats, minor skirmishes and challenges. It also uses dopamine to give a sense of achievement and accomplishment once the dust settles. But this hormonal cocktail also encourages bonding and connections with others; it's not all about fight or flight! The last outcome helps us support each other, share knowledge and resources when under pressure. This opens us up to the possibility of a more nuanced response to the stress hormones, beyond the fight, flight, freeze, flop or fawn responses. Now doesn't that feel like a healthier alternative view when it comes to handling stress?

The Vagus Nerve

In 1994, Dr Stephen Porges put forward a theory called the Polyvagal Theory,[8] explaining the importance of the vagus nerve in supporting emotional regulation, social connection and the fear response in humans. He called it the social engagement system, and it helps us navigate relationships. The vagus nerve is the longest set of cranial nerves running from the brain stem through the face and throat, past the heart to the digestive system. Dr Porges' theory stated this was an evolutionary adaptation to help us deal with trauma by encouraging the formation of social bonds or networks when under threat. Perhaps the vagus nerve is part of the tend-and-befriend process.

The Fight-and-flight Response and the Rest-and-digest Response

The autonomic nervous system contains three strands: the sympathetic nervous system helps us to respond to threat (alarm on); the parasympathetic nervous system helps us to rest and digest (alarm off); and the enteric nervous system controls gastrointestinal functions.

The body can only be in one of two states: fight and flight (alarm on) or rest and digest (alarm off). When our internal alarm is switched on, we are in fight mode, our survival response. When the danger is over we chill and relax, rest and digest. But this only happens once we feel safe and secure. The problem with those who experience ongoing stress is that they lose the ability to find the off switch, and confuse the messages the body is trying to give them.

The purpose of this book is to help you navigate a safe way beyond the confusion of messages from the brain so you are not in a constant state of high alert.

Why Thoughts Lead to Stress

The brain's job is to think. It churns out thoughts like a factory production line; inevitably, some are fantastic, some are neutral and some are just rubbish; but that's okay because most of the time our logical brain can filter them out. Like any good gardener, it weeds out the gobbledegook, but a few weeds can sneak in. Sometimes a nonsensical thought can command our attention, introduce doubt and make us worry, even when we know those thoughts are outlandish. This is more likely to happen when we are feeling a bit under par, rundown or overworked.

What complicates the process further is that thoughts can lie to us. We have cognitive distortions and biases – our mind is sneaky! It has a way of getting rid of things that don't match our current belief systems in an effort to minimise uncertainty. The mind likes familiar routines, even when they are not good for us. As long as we maintain a predictable 'safe' world, it's happy deleting, distorting and generalizing information to fit our world view. Great if you live by yourself on an island and do not want any relationships, but we are surrounded by other thinking humans with their unique world view, so disagreements and clashes are inevitable.

How Is 'Stress' Different from 'Anxiety'?

We tend to use these words interchangeably, but they are not the same thing. Stress is the body's evolutionary physical and biological response, involving the release of stress hormones for energy and to promote action. Scientists can detect the biomarkers of stress hormones in the bloodstream and alpha-amylase in saliva. The stress response automatically turns on when we feel threatened and turns off when the crisis is over.

Anxiety is the emotion that reminds us to be vigilant to danger, to solve the crisis, to stay alert and aware until life-threatening situations have passed. But if we find it impossible to switch off anxiety when the danger has passed, that traps us in an unhealthy loop that re-triggers the stress response, and anxiety becomes an illness called 'anxiety disorder'.

When you are in a loop, it's hard to tell which comes first: the chicken or the egg, the stress response or the anxiety? Understanding how this self-perpetuating loop works is the first step towards breaking the cycle.

What Happens Inside the Body When We Are Stressed

A lot of changes take place inside the body when we register a potential threat and get that jolt of stress energy to act quickly to save our lives. The more it persists, the more you are likely to experience some physical reactions. Take a look at the list opposite, and the box on page 50, and make a note in your notebook if you have experienced these symptoms at work or at home.

- Aches and pains
- Anxiety or depression
- Break out of rashes, itchy skin
- Tight chest
- Clenched jaw
- Cold, sweaty hands
- Dry throat or mouth
- Eye problems (blurry, tunnel vision or eye pain)
- Fertility problems (menstrual cycle stops)
- Heartburn
- High blood sugar, leading to type 2 diabetes
- Infections
- Loss of appetite
- Loss of hair
- Migraine, tension headache
- More toilet breaks
- Nausea, upset stomach or other digestive issues (ulcers, irritable bowel syndrome, gas, constipation, diarrhoea)
- Racing heart, high blood pressure (you might be on medication for this)
- Rapid, shallow breathing
- Sexual problems (low sex drive or erectile dysfunction)
- Shaking or trembling (jelly legs or hands)
- Skin problems (itchy skin, rashes, flare up of eczema, psoriasis, etc.)
- Sleep problems (insomnia)
- Sweating
- Tense muscles along the spine (protects the spinal cord)

The short-term, positive result of stress hormones being released during fight-or-flight is our increased physical ability and focus. But these reactions are not designed to be experienced long term so, when they are, it is not surprising they adversely affect our health. Whether this range of symptoms happens to you, depends on how you handle the stress.

The Effects of Stress on Your Body

Head	Chest
• Dry mouth	• Breathing fast
• Blushing	• Breathing shallow
• Feelings of danger	• Hyper-ventilating
• Confusion	• Chest pains
• Sense of detachment	• Tingling sensations
• Feeling faint, dizzy or light-headed	• Fast heartbeat
• Tunnel vision	• Palpitations
• Sharper or blurred vision	• High blood pressure
	• Fast pulse
Digestive system	**Limbs**
• Butterflies	• Sweaty palms
• Diarrhoea	• Cold hands
• Feeling nauseous	• Tingling, trembling or numbness
• Indigestion	• Tension
• Urge to urinate	• Aching or painful muscles
• Churning sensations in the stomach	

Threat or challenge?

Researchers continue to look at the long-term outcome of viewing situations as a threat or a challenge. Research by Mark D. Seery[9] highlighted that although both can lead to the heart beating faster and harder, when a situation is viewed as a challenge there is a positive effect on the arteries – they dilate more and allow a freer flow of blood – whereas in threat mode, the arteries narrow and less blood is pumped. Challenge responses therefore increase the efficiency of the heart system, which could give positive effects.

The Thought Emotion Action Cycle (TEA Cycle™)

There is a connection between what we think, feel and do. If you live with a thought for long enough it will spark a feeling – it's the mind's way of mapping out more meaningful data and enriching an experience. Another thought might occur as a result, which sparks yet another feeling. Eventually, the tension between the thoughts and feelings give rise to action, a behaviour that moves us away or towards a desired goal. What we end up doing could be part of a positive or negative pattern cycle.

The stress response is our innate survival mechanism, but it can perpetuate a chain of negative thoughts, emotions and actions that keep us stuck in a negative cycle.

Imagine being able to take a snapshot of an event, then having the opportunity to analyse what went wrong and fix it? The TEA Cycle helps you imagine, visualize and verbalize the consequences of not changing action. It helps deepen an awareness of the thoughts, emotions or actions we naturally feel when overwhelmed, stressed and under pressure.

Unintended consequences can be tracked using the TEA Cycle. This simple system, which I created during my work with clients, is based on a cognitive behavioural therapy (CBT) concept. It helps us to question whether the event is really the problem, or whether it's our interpretation, perspective and thinking. I use a memorable acronym, TEA, to take a snapshot of the vicious cycle, deconstruct the elements we want to change, and reconstruct a positive reward cycle using new elements that create the desired outcome.

THE TEA CYCLE

What triggers your stress cycle?

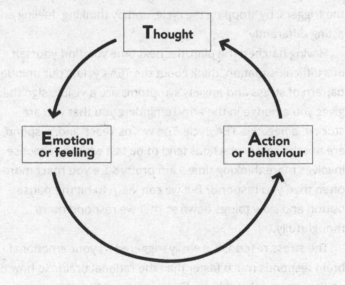

Having a system not only helps you conserve precious energy and resources, it also helps you avoid embarrassment from overreacting or reacting too quickly. Once it becomes instinctive, you will no longer revert to the negative cycle by default – because you will have a plan B!

The first phase of the TEA Cycle is to look in more detail at your negative cycle. What actually happens in stressful situations: what do you think, feel and do? Then you have to come up with alternatives to change the outcome by avoiding the triggers, by stopping the cycle, and by thinking, feeling and acting differently.

Having hatched the plan, the next time you find yourself in a difficult situation, think about the TEA Cycle. Your unique pattern of stress and anxiety symptoms are a visible sign that gives you a nudge in the arm, reminding you that you are stuck in a negative TEA Cycle. The words 'react' and 'respond' are not the same, reactions tend to be fast while a response involves more thinking time. I am pretty sure you react more often than you respond? But we can learn to hit the pause button and slow things down so that we respond more thoughtfully.

The stress response is easily triggered as your emotional brain responds much faster than the rational brain. So how do you put your rational brain back in charge? Try changing your breathing pattern. Breathe steadily and deeply in and out a few times, concentrating on filling your lungs, then emptying them as much as you can. This is all you have to do to trigger the body's natural relaxation response. Another thing to try is shaking it out, as we saw on page 28.

Now use your rational brain to get things back on track by calling on your senses to help you challenge the reality of any danger. Ask yourself 'Am I really in danger? Is there a wild animal, fire, flood or earthquake?' Hopefully the answer is no, and your senses can feed back this reassuring information to your brain. This simple observation can help tone down the intensity of the stress response and set you on a whole new path.

New thinking then helps you reconstruct a positive TEA Cycle. Substitute more helpful elements that could break the old ways of thinking, feeling and doing. Can you think of an alternative thought that calms the situation? What feeling would be the result of thinking this? What action would be the result of this feeling?

An alternative approach to reconstructing the positive cycle is asking yourself what you would like to feel, what thought would this create and what action would result.

EXERCISE: Learn to Use the TEA Cycle System

Use the TEA Cycle to help deconstruct a problem that triggers your stress response. For example, you may find going into work stressful if you have had problems with a colleague.

- Write down the Thoughts you are having about the situation. Leave a space underneath as you will come back to this.
- Then write down the Emotions you are feeling, with a space beneath. If the emotion is from the fear group – anxiety, worry, concern, doubt, 'what if' –

you may have physical anxiety symptoms, such as racing heart, sweating, churning stomach. Make a note of these too.

- Finally, write down the Actions you took.
- Go through each one again and think about the consequences in each case and write them down under your TEA Cycle headings.
- Finally, change to a different colour pen and go back again and challenge your thinking, interrogate it. You might need a couple of rounds to connect more dots and gather the data. What other thoughts could you have had? What emotions would they have led to? What else could you have done?
- Also think about the consequence of having a TEA Cycle like this – but not doing anything to actively change it.

You are likely to have more than one alternative, and that's reassuring when problem solving.

Stress Energy Assessment

Now you have read this chapter, rerun your Stress Energy Assessments (pages 14–15), applying your new understanding, and fill in your progress graph.

EXERCISE: The TEA Cycle Table

Copy the format of this TEA Cycle table in your notebook and use it when you want to reconstruct a situation to give you the results you want.

TEA Cycle	Negative TEA Cycle	Consequences	Positive TEA Cycle	Consequences
Situation	What circumstances are you in?	How could you avoid being in those circumstances?	What could you do instead?	What would happen as a result?
Stressors	What starts the negative stress cycle?	How could you avoid that trigger?	Can you replace negative with positive triggers?	What would happen as a result?
Thoughts	What are you thinking?	What are the consequences of thinking that way?	How else could you think about the situation?	What would happen as a result?
Emotions	How does that make you feel?	What are the consequences of feeling that way?	What other feelings could you experience?	What would happen as a result?
Actions	How do you behave as a result?	What are the consequences of those actions?	What else could you do?	What would happen as a result?
How does your body react?	What physical symptoms do you experience?	What did you do about them?	Could you try coping with stress-related symptoms in a different way, such as breathing exercises?	What would happen as a result?

3

UNDERSTANDING YOUR STRESS ENERGY

The universe is made up of constantly changing energy, which provides the building blocks of life for everything, from our bodies to the chair you are sitting on or the food you eat. Energy is created by the tiniest movement of electrons within each atom. (We used to think electrons were the smallest particles until quantum physicists discovered quarks.) The vibrational frequency matters. If they vibrate slowly, then things appear more solid; if they vibrate quickly, then things are more fluid (liquids and gases). The chair you might be sitting on right this minute is vibrating; it does so extremely slowly and so remains solid.

Our bodies are made up of the same energy and it powers everything we do, conscious or unconscious. That includes not only the physical side of our body's activity – breathing, moving, seeing – but thinking, feeling and emotions too. Our feelings are, in essence, waves of invisible energy in motion, e-motion. Emotional energy (for example love, anger, excitement), physical energy (illness, aches and pain) and spiritual energy (zoning out, intuition and going within).

Try to imagine thoughts and emotions as this vibrational energy and compare love energy with fear energy. You might say love energy is a positive, light energy, vibrating at a high frequency that can raise your level of excitement or joy with positive thoughts and actions. Fear energy, on the other hand, feels heavy, slow and negative, vibrating at a much lower frequency, and pulling you down and making you feel frustrated, annoyed, sad, guilty or angry. You might notice that an energy has a physical as well as an emotional impact.

Let's review some of the knowledge we have amassed so far and start to weave the complex strands together.

There are many different types of energy that make us think, feel and act in different ways. Use your TEA Cycle to embrace the high-frequency energy around and within you.

What is Stress Energy?

The original concept of stress comes from the world of physics and describes the strain on materials: how much pressure can you put on a plank of wood before it breaks? We have transferred it to apply to human thoughts and emotions and the behaviour that results from that pressure, or stress, we find ourselves under. We can use our imagination to understand the concept of stress and how it relates to our thoughts, emotions and actions.

Talking about stress in this way has been helpful for me and my coaching clients, and I have worked on the concept under the influence of research from respected cell biologist and epigeneticist Bruce Lipton, brain specialist Daniel Amen and health psychologist Kelly McGonigal.

Human beings experience stress as an inevitable part of life. We have seen that the brain and the body are constantly scanning for internal changes or external environmental problems that we might need to respond to. This is stress energy, evolved to keep us alive and safe from woolly mammoths! The problem is that we have become used to regarding stress as one-sided.

Stress is Not One-dimensional

The prevailing idea that the only time we experience stress energy is when we are under threat of danger does not make sense in the 21st century. Life for us is complicated and there are far too many stressors out there, but they are not all bad, and even the bad ones are annoying in different degrees. Countless life events – from small things such as being late for work, to major things such as getting married, buying a new home or getting a promotion – exert some kind of pressure on our lives but it is not necessarily negative.

Think about the definition we started with from physics: the levels of pressure we can exert on a plank of wood. Small degrees of pressure would have no effect; a bit more pressure might compress the wood and even make it stronger. Then move beyond this, add more and more and it will eventually snap.

Stress cannot therefore be defined as entirely bad – or good. If stress really was that awful, none of us would make it past the age of 20, having worried about every little blip in life. We wouldn't progress in our jobs, and we'd certainly never move house or have a family! If stress was always bad, why do the majority of performers, athletes and business people survive and thrive on it? How do musicians, dancers, actors and singers use their stress energy to enhance their performances?

Viewing every event as a threat is not helpful or realistic. It will simply send us into a negative spiral, worrying that we don't have the resources to cope. And if we allow every minor stressor to get to us, then it will be self-fulfilling and we will have more problems than we can cope with.

The Power of Language

Part of this process is defining the level of threat, and that is where language becomes important. The English language is renowned for its subtlety. Sometimes we couldn't even explain why one word is better than another in a particular context, but each word carries with it such nuances of meaning that it can make a huge difference. Anger, rage, fury, ire, wrath are all from the same family of emotions yet different, with each one demanding a different threat response.

When we are careless and lazy with language, we accidentally generate more of the stress we are trying to avoid. As a simple example, think about the words 'drizzling', 'raining', 'pouring', 'pelting down'. If we only used 'raining' for all those occasions, we'd have no idea whether it's a light shower, a downpour or a monsoon. In stress terms, it helps to know the level of a stress reaction otherwise we could misinterpret how to deal with it.

Accurately label your emotions: anger, strain, curiosity, mild irritation, anxiety, annoyance, pressure, frustration, contemplation. By so doing we can avoid having the same extreme fear response to non-threatening life events.

Precision matters when you are talking to your brain. Be careful what you say to it, as it is easily programmed with a negative idea and it's always listening. Language exists for a reason, and by being precise you help your brain, heart and gut decide exactly how to manage the triggered stress energy.

Unless you practise this skill, you are harming your mental wellbeing. Do words really matter? Yes. Imagine calling all the different types of cheese in the world by one word, 'cheese', instead of defining them as hard or soft, Brie or Cheddar, and so on. What would happen if you tried to communicate your shopping list to the person behind the deli counter? Imagine going into your local car dealership and asking for a red car, without stating the make or model; the sales person would have a hard time helping you.

Another way of grading the stress threat is by size: small, medium, large, extra large. It's simple but effective, and stops the 'all or nothing' thinking habit.

Language matters, and it has the ability to alter your emotional mood for better or worse. Once you realize that thoughts are connected to what you feel, you will stop classifying the majority of situations you encounter as 'dangerous'. I came across the phrase 'daily hassles' and it seemed another sound way to describe and grade the annoying life events that we all experience at the bottom end of the stress scale.

Stress Energy Pathways

When I work with this concept, I imagine my stress energy following three different pathways.

- **Threat energy** deals with real physical danger, it makes you stronger and does its job well. However, it can be a low-frequency energy, which leads to lower performance and poorer spontaneous decisions.
- **Challenge energy** takes over if there is no physical threat and helps us to analyse and problem solve. It has a higher frequency and can modify the hormones activated by the stress response, leading to higher performance, greater accuracy and better co-ordination.
- **Tend-and-befriend or connection energy** helps us to reconnect with others and reach out for more resources or to give help to others.

Perceiving every situation as a threat keeps us locked in the negative cycle of anxiety and fear, which keeps re-triggering our stress response. The way to approach stress in the 21st century is to open up other pathways. Learn to deal with stress energy by repurposing threat energy and reframing it positively. When we choose to change threat energy into challenge energy, we open up a whole new set of possibilities. Even more possibilities open up if we can channel that energy not only to step up to challenges but also to reach out and seek or give support to others.

We will do that using the TEA Cycle principles and also introduce another system called NUTS, a process developed by Dr Sonia Lupien. Using these two systems, you will gradually become more confident in trusting yourself. You will learn not to overreact to threat energy until you have assessed and defined it. Then you will be able to use the more relevant stress energy pathway to solve problems and pull out resources or create new ones.

How to Switch from One Pathway to Another

So our life experience is full of all degrees of stress, and we need to be more nuanced than just reacting with fight-or-flight. We do have the power to shift from the instinctive anxiety-inducing feelings of fear and threat to a more empowering, active and inspiring energy.

Scientific evidence shows there are subtle changes in the combination of stress hormones depending on how we assess any potential danger. Plus, through a process called neuroplasticity, the brain has the ability to break habits and patterns and form new brain networks that deal with situations in better ways. Use your earlier assessment to re-examine example situations and notice whether there was an alternative to the threat pathway.

First, do a reality check on the situation – is it really a threat: wild animals, fire, flood or earthquake? Always use all your senses to detect and define threat levels – any life-threatening situation is likely to be seen, smelt, tasted, heard or felt. Our skin is important here; the largest organ in the body is designed to protect us from external threats and spot danger. If this is a dangerous situation, it's not always necessary to be totally calm. Stress energy also helps us stay alert, focused and have more strength to take action or to run.

Second, consider whether you have the capacity to deal with the issue. What skills and resources do you need? How will you apply them to resolving the problem?

If you can't find a resolution on your own, who would you reach out for to support you?

EXERCISE: Redirecting my Stress Energy

Think of a situation that you found stressful, or imagine one if you prefer. Write notes on what happened when you followed the threat pathway. What were the consequences? Then see how you could have dealt with it using the alternative positive pathways.

- **Threat:** Pathway 1 deals with real danger. Is the situation truly a threat?
- **Challenge:** Pathway 2 does not represent a threat and you have the skills and resources to deal with it.
- **Tend and befriend:** Pathway 3 shows there is still a challenge but requires you to connect with others to enlist the skills and resources required; or to support others.

The more you do this exercise, the more you will reject the threat pathway and turn your stress energy into a positive force.

You can develop this strategy using the TEA Cycle, taking some time to notice the uncomfortable stress signals in your mind (negative thoughts) and body (physiological sensations) that are activated by a stressful situation. This will help you go through the stages and to learn when you need to stop and reflect.

EXERCISE: Applying the TEA Cycle to Change a Threat to a Challenge

Using the TEA Cycle (page 57), make notes on a situation that didn't go according to plan because you only used your threat energy. You might like to choose something involving a presentation: you may use a work scenario, having to make a speech at a wedding or just introducing yourself to a new neighbour.

- What is the situation? How could you avoid or modify it?
- What are the triggers that make you feel stressed? How could you side step or change them?
- **Thoughts:** what are you thinking? What are the consequences of thinking that way? How else could you think?
- **Emotions:** what are you feeling? What are the consequences? How would changing your thinking change how you feel?

- **Actions:** what do you do? How can you change that? What else could you do?

You may like to think about how a performer (actor, singer, dancer, musician) you admire would utilize their challenge energy to cope with the situation. Many performers are naturally shy people but adept at harnessing their positive energy.

Role Models

Another way to help you with this task is to think about how other people deal with events by turning them into challenges. Some people do this quite naturally. We won't see them going around negatively brain-washing themselves by telling themselves they are stressed out. They will have experienced the same surge of threat energy during a crisis as you, but they pause and analyse, then repurpose the energy to confidently meet the challenge. They also know how to enlist the right resources or people for support. If it's something they can't do by themselves, they ask for help – it's not a dirty word, it's a sensible strategy.

If we dare to find the courage to change our assumptions that stress is always bad, we can learn to make better life choices and use the energy from a situation to improve our performance.

Are You NUTS?

Before we move on, I want to introduce another technique to help you understand what triggers your stress; it's NUTS!

How strongly we react to stressful situations is entirely personal as it depends on our own life experiences, our resilience and the circumstances of the situation.

Dr Sonia Lupien, founder and director of the Centre for Studies on Human Stress,[10] identified the concept of defining the potentially stress-inducing elements of any situation and gave it the acronym NUTS.

- **N** indicates the presence of novelty, doing something different that is outside of your normal routine.
- **U** indicates unpredictability, the moments when we really haven't got a clue what's going to happen next.
- **T** represents the fear of physical or psychological threat to our bodies or our ego, which essentially manages our personality, identity, self-esteem, reputation and how we view ourselves.
- **S** represents our desire for a sense of control, feeling in control is the gateway to calm confidence, and losing control is the gateway to stress.

We can use NUTS to help us assess stressful situations on a scale of 1 to 10, where 1=low stress and 10=high, and change our resultant stress energy by thinking how we can make a situation less novel, more predictable, less threatening or create a greater sense of control.

The real skill to having a healthy life where stress is regarded as normal, is to understand how to assess the level of threat and the three stress energy pathways open to you so you take a realistic approach to life's problems.

EXERCISE: Using NUTS to Deconstruct and Reconstruct Stress

Pick a situation and write it in your notebook if one of the NUTS elements of stress applies. Think about how you could lower your stress. Try it with different situations.

- **N:** new – you have never dealt with this before.
- **U:** unpredictable – there is inherent uncertainty in the situation.
- **T:** threat to the ego – the part that controls our personality, identity, reputation.
- **S:** sense of control – how much do you have?

This will help you target the decisions and changes you can make when dealing with situations you find difficult.

Stress Energy Assessment

Now you have read this chapter, rerun your Stress Energy Assessments (pages 14–15), applying your new understanding, and fill in your progress graph.

4

IDENTIFYING YOUR TRIGGERS

We can only solve a problem when we have the full picture, so – having established some background – let's move on with the critical step of identifying your unique triggers, or stressors; this is a key skill to navigating stress and managing your stress energy.

As we have seen, automatic scanning for threat is a great starting place, but problems arise when your subconscious is overzealous and you react to minor annoyances in the same way you do for real dangers.

We have also emphasised that stress is individual and each person has their own specific triggers, or stressors, that freak them out. They may be external triggers – responses to what is going on in your surroundings – or they may be internal triggers – self-esteem issues, internal self-talk issues or other problems in your emotional or psychological profile. You need to identify those triggers.

A problem arises when you react to minor annoyances in the same way you do for real dangers.

Let's start by looking broadly at the types of external trigger you are already aware of. Are you confident at work but get very nervous in social situations? Is it being accepted or rejected by others that you worry about, or something else? For the next exercise, we will define triggers broadly to help you understand which type of trigger is most difficult for you.

EXERCISE: Acknowledge Types of Stress Triggers

Later we will identify your stressors more specifically. For now, write in your notebook the areas of your life that you know stress you out. You might want to fill in a bit more detail, particularly giving several example of the stressors you identify.

- Situations at work or at home
- Social situations (cinema, restaurant)
- Activities
- People (co-workers, partners, family)
- Places (crowds, open spaces)
- Times of day
- Seasons

If you have included enough examples, you should see a pattern emerging of similar stress-inducing events.

Regular journaling helps you capture details at specific moments. It gives you the opportunity to get stuff out of your head. Jot down how you really think, feel and behave so that you can return to it when you are not feeling stressed and observe and analyse the problem from a less emotionally charged place. That is the time to apply your TEA Cycle thinking.

Meeting Our Needs and Fear of Loss

When something really matters to us, when it is valuable or essential, we are more likely to get stressed at the thought of losing it. Let's think about the things that matter to us – family, friends, children, home, money, job, health, hobbies, rest and relaxation, pets, holidays. The level of our stress and anxiety matches the degree to which we care and fear the loss of it.

Underpinning that degree of care is what psychologists define by referring to Maslow's hierarchy of needs,[11] written in 1943. It can help to explain why some things feel threatening and others do not.

The hierarchy uses a pyramid-shaped model to explain the psychology behind human motivation. Maslow put forward the idea that there are five universal levels of need that we ascend as and when we meet the previous criteria. These can be categorized as basic, psychological and self-fulfilment needs and, like a computer game or the board game snakes and ladders, we can tumble back due to unexpected circumstances.

- **Level 1 is your physiological needs:** Do you have water, air, food, shelter, sleep, clothing, reproduction?
- **Level 2 covers safety needs:** Are you safe and secure? Do you have a stable environment and protection from danger?
- **Level 3 is about love and belonging:** We all need intimacy, friendships, family and a sense of connection.
- **Level 4 is our need for self-esteem:** This covers our status and recognition in a social context, our sense of self-worth,

mutual respect from those around us and acceptance of who we are.

- **Level 5 is self-actualisation:** The top level is being the best that you can be, using creativity, acceptance, spontaneity, purpose and meaning.

If our needs are not met, this can be a trigger for stress, both mental and physical. At a basic level 1, the consequences of not meeting our needs are likely to be physical. If we are cold, hungry and homeless, our stress levels will be high. Those basic needs have to be met before we can move up the hierarchy. Almost anything could be a trigger for you.

If you have moved up to level 2, you are likely to have a different set of triggers. Potential threats could make it difficult to focus on any higher-level need and even force you to take a step backwards.

As you move up the hierarchy, more of your needs are being met, so stressors should become fewer and less threatening.

Remember that any trigger has the potential to be positive or negative, and even threats we assess as negative can be turned around.

Holmes and Rahe Stress Scale

In 1967, psychiatrists Thomas Holmes and Richard Rahe defined a hierarchy of stressful events in order to try to predict the future impact of stress on the development of ill health. It surveyed responses from 5,000 patients about 43 life events encountered over the previous two years, awarding a 'life-change unit' according to how many times it was mentioned by participants. The hierarchy was updated in 2006 to cover more questions (55 instead of 43).

Although standardized for age, gender, race and religion, no account was made for the following variables: different cultural interpretations and moral values, coping abilities and resources, resilience and stress tolerance, and life goals and personality. We should also take into account life was different in 1967. The life-change questions reflected a generation with different values, work ethics and social environments.[12]

EXERCISE: Top 18 Stressful Life Events

Here are the top 18 stressors according to Holmes and Rahe to give you an idea of the sort of thing that affects other people. Tick any that apply to you. Define them as internal or external (I or E), then as positive or negative (P or N).

- Death of a spouse (100 units)
- Divorce (73)
- Marital separation (65)
- Jail term (63)
- Death of a close family member (63)
- Personal injury or illness (53)
- Marriage (50)
- Loss of job (47)
- Marital reconciliation (45)
- Retirement (45)
- Change in health of a family member (44)
- Pregnancy (40)
- Sexual problems (39)
- Gain of a new family member (44)
- Business readjustment (39)
- Change in financial state (38)
- Death of a close friend (37)
- Change to a different line of work (36)

The more you have ticked, the more you have to cope with in terms of stress levels. However, if you are working on your recognition of your stressors and directing your stress energy into positive pathways, you will have the ability to be as happy and positive as someone with fewer pressures.

External and Internal Stressors

Another way to define the stressors in our lives is to divide them into external and internal. Like invisible trip wires just waiting to catch us out, stressors change through the decades, and 21st-century living means we have a different set of stressors from our parents and previous generations, despite the tougher physical and mental hardships they faced. The trip wires are everywhere, although you should always keep reminding yourself that they can be negative or positive in varying degrees.

- **External stressors:** Environmental stressors are those we find in our surroundings or social situations.
- **Internal stressors:** These include anything that is happening inside your body, such as physical or mental illness.

We have looked at several lists of stressors and combined them to define these five major stressor groups: environment, relationships, work, money and health. Many topics overlap across the five groups.

The Get-on-with-it Generation

Negative overthinking is more of a modern phenomenon. I can cite examples of people in my own family who understand the power of positive thinking and reject negative self-programming. My British mother-in-law was born in the mid-1930s, and always said her mum and grandma didn't call all the difficulties they encountered stress, they simply 'got on with it' and 'figured things out'. My Jamaican parents are equally hardy, and simply get on with things too.

EXERCISE: What is Stressing You?

Your stress triggers are personal to you.

- Look at the list above and make a note in your notebook of the things that are affecting you. Group them under the headings: environment, relationships, work, money and health.
- Add any other things that are personal to you or change the headings to suit your life.
- Review the groups under which you have listed the items in the most relevant way to you. See if you can see a pattern emerging. What is it that stresses you the most?

It may be clear that one area of your life is most in need of attention.

Environmental Stressors

Environmental stressors can be anything from living conditions to broader issues of your neighbourhood or the political landscape, social issues or climate change. Some of the broader aspects of these are certainly beyond the efforts of one individual to change, but there is always something you can lend your voice to. Don't give up just because you feel there is nothing you can do about big issues, such as child or animal cruelty, right this moment – there is always something you could do about it in the future by campaigning and joining like-minded organisations.

- **Economic and political issues:** Local or national politics, personal safety, neighbourhood watch.
- **World issues:** Climate change, wars, natural disasters, pandemics.

Look at the impact Greta Thunberg has had on the climate-change discussion if you need an example of how one individual can have a big impact on a huge issue.

EXERCISE: Examine Your Environmental Triggers

If you have identified triggers in this category, investigate further to see if you could handle them in a different way.

- Make a note of any environmental triggers.
- Use your TEA Cycle to investigate one representative incident.

There are other ways to divert your stress down a positive channel, even if the stress trigger is outside your control. For example. if you are worried about climate change, you could try doing more recycling at home or join an environmental group.

COVID-19 and Political Division

To demonstrate how environmental factors affect people's stress levels, the American Psychological Association reviewed the main causes of stress in January 2021.[13] It fell about a year into the COVID-19 pandemic and immediately after the inauguration of Joe Biden as president (replacing Donald Trump). The primary causes of stress were listed as the state of the nation, the coronavirus pandemic and political unrest.

By comparison, the major stressors in 2014, about halfway through the Obama administration, were money, health, relationships, poor nutrition, media overload and sleep deprivation.

Relationship Stressors

We are fascinated with one another's lives, and reality TV shows prove this. Human beings are social creatures with a strong desire to be accepted and to fit in, to receive and give love, and ultimately to procreate to keep the species going. We are drawn to being part of a community, team or tribe and are careful not to fall out with them – harking back to the past when group protection ensured survival. We gravitate towards making connections, no matter how permanent or fleeting they are – at work, school, in social settings, and even on a trip to the corner shop.

Relationships can be a huge source of joy, but they can be a significant source of stress if they are going wrong. Relationship stress triggers might include:

- **Partners:** Divorce or relationship problems, sexual problems, betrayal, abuse, poor communication, arguments, poor physical or mental health.
- **Children:** Behavioural and learning problems, stepchildren (blended families), issues at school, exams and studies, boyfriends and girlfriends.
- **Family:** Cultural issues, illness, caring duties, bereavement (people and pets), familial pressure.

- **Friends and co-workers:** Disagreements, problems with colleagues, bullying.

EXERCISE: Examine Your Relationship Triggers

If you have identified triggers in this category, investigate further to see if you could handle them in a different way.

- Make a note of any relationship issues that are causing you concern.
- Try not to muddle issues – although some may be inextricably linked.
- Use your TEA Cycle to investigate one representative incident. If you find yourself getting emotional, stop until you are feeling more relaxed and able to be objective.

Think about your ultimate goal and try to realign your thinking and actions in a more positive way.

Work Stressors

Work brings plenty of opportunity for doing the things that we love, for expressing our gifts, talents and skills – as well as bringing in money to live – but unfortunately we don't all have the dream job, and work can be a major source of stress, reducing our confidence and self-esteem or creating physical and mental illness.

> The World Health Organisation defines job stress as: 'The response people have when presented with work demands and pressures that are not matched to their knowledge and abilities and which challenge their ability to cope.'

We spend so much time at work that it can begin to merge with our identity to the point that when we socialize we introduce ourselves by our names followed by our job titles. If we lose our jobs, get demoted, or are made redundant, it can be devastating as it feels as though we've lost part of our identity.

A major issue at work can be confusing job stress with job challenges. Challenging work energizes us on a physical and psychological level; it can motivate and help us learn new skills to do our jobs well. As we overcome a challenge, we get a sense of accomplishment and can relax. How often have you left work feeling you've made a positive and worthwhile contribution that boosts your self-esteem and self-worth? At the opposite extreme, the challenges can become unrealistically demanding and we feel ill-equipped to perform them. The positive feelings evaporate, setting the stage for job dissatisfaction, chronic stress, injury and illness.

Another common issue is dealing with other people's work ethics and habits. If you are always on time to meetings, for example, it can be infuriating if others are not punctual.

Work stressors often include:

- **Overworking:** Time spent at work, unsocial hours, heavy workload, unrealistic expectations.
- **Insecurity:** Redundancy or threat of job loss, zero hours contracts.
- **Lack of confidence:** New job, lack of training.
- **Frustration:** Thwarted ambition, lack of opportunity, unfairness, lack of organisation, boredom, conflict.
- **Poor conditions:** Insufficient personal space or facilities and equipment.
- **Personal aspects:** Un-co-operative co-workers, supervisor, boss, discrimination, harassment, loss of motivation and enthusiasm for tasks, lack of personal development training and growth.

Mega-stressful Jobs

Some jobs are recognized as being more stressful than others because they take a personal toll on wellbeing or disrupt relationships and family lives. They may be dangerous, dirty, involve conflict or aggressive members of the public, witness death or distress, carry a high level of personal risk or personal injury and more.

Think about your job and whether it is defined as particularly stressful. If it is, then you will need to learn quickly how to manage your threat, challenge and support systems (see page 66).

EXERCISE: Examine Your Work Triggers

If you have identified triggers in this category, investigate further to see if you could handle them in a different way.

- Make a note of any work-related stress triggers.
- Use your TEA Cycle to investigate one representative incident.
- Try to see things from both sides, especially if colleagues are involved.

You may decide that you need to talk with a colleague or the boss; try to do so without blaming others, and acknowledge that, if changes are needed, they must happen on both sides.

Exhaustion and Burnout

The ultimate response to your negative stress experience is likely to be chronic stress and burnout, affecting both physical and mental aspects of your life. This is most often caused when a major aspect of our lives – usually work – takes over every aspect of pleasure. We have a work culture in which overworking is worn as a badge of honour, with an average working week of 40 to 44 hours globally. Even if you arrive early, it might be frowned upon if you leave on time. Unfortunately, excessive hours working in the office or from home does not equal higher productivity. At around 50 hours, productivity declines markedly so the extra hours are not well spent.

Physical signs can be tiredness, irritability, loss of motivation and enjoyment. Other potential health problems include headaches, stomach problems, depression and anxiety, damage to blood vessels, higher blood pressure which increases risk of heart problems or a stroke, and sleep issues. If you maintain this level of pressure, you will reach a breaking point where chronic stress will become your norm. Your body will increasingly show stress symptoms that it can't turn off and that will negatively impact your organs, immune system and general health.

Please note that 'rust out', feeling bored and under-challenged is also a stressful issue.

In the next chapter, we will look in more detail at how to arrest this process and establish a better work/life balance.

Money Stressors

We all need enough money coming into our households to cover our basic needs and, hopefully, allow us a certain quality of life. There is no doubt that the distribution of wealth in the world is unfair and, even in our Western society, there is still a big gap between rich and poor. The most critical financial worries that we experience relate to having enough to cover the basics – food, warmth and shelter. For others there might be budgeting issues – finding it hard to allocate a monthly salary sensibly. For a smaller group there may be issues of gambling or other addictions.

Financial stressor may include:

Budgeting: Debt, mortgage or rent, education, insufficient funds, not able to keep to a budget.

Work: Poorly paid, loss of work, zero hours contracts, high travel costs.

Unexpected expenses: New addition to the family, major repairs or other outgoings.

Never ignore financial problems. They will only get worse if you try to deny their existence. Seek advice from family, friends or specialist agencies.

EXERCISE: Examine Your Financial Triggers

If you have identified triggers in this category, investigate further to see if you could handle them in a different way. It may be appropriate to ask for help and support, especially if you are in debt. Never delay seeking help.

> - Make a note of any money-related stress triggers.
> - Use your TEA Cycle to investigate one representative incident.
> - It may be that you will need help to deal with your problem.
>
> Getting to the source of the problem is key here as until the issues are dealt with in a practical sense, the stress will remain.

Health Stressors

Suffering from poor health, especially chronic conditions, is a huge drain on energy that can lead to further problems. You may be able to add to the following list and make it personal to you.

- **Ill-health:** Physical or mental health of self or loved ones, caring for elderly parents, growing old, low self-esteem.
- **Bereavement:** Loss of family or friends or pets.
- **Abuse:** Physical or mental, substance abuse, addiction.
- **Environment:** toxic atmosphere, food additives, allergies, pollen.

EXERCISE: Examine Your Health Triggers

If you have identified triggers in this category, investigate further to see if you could handle them in a different way.

- Make a note of any health-related stress triggers.
- Use your TEA Cycle to investigate one representative incident.
- It may be that you will need help to deal with your problem.

Getting to the source of the problem is key here as until the issues are dealt with in a practical sense, the stress will remain.

Internal Mind Stressors: Automatic Negative Thoughts (ANTs)

As well as the external triggers we have been looking at, we are also subject to internal triggers from negative thinking patterns that impact our mental and emotional health. These comprise automatic negative thoughts (ANTs) and negative self-talk. They drive stress and keep us locked in negative TEA Cycles.

Our brain is like a factory production line churning out thoughts 24 hours a day, quickly and automatically, some positive, some negative. Among those thoughts are automatic negative thoughts. We take notice of them, as we should as they may signify danger. However, because they are automatic, we don't always interrogate or stop to evaluate them correctly. Sometimes we simply assume that something is true because we have thought it, but that is not always the case. Our thoughts tell lies.

When the stress response is triggered in our brain, we can respond or we can react – you may recall these sound similar but are subtly different courses of action. Reacting quickly without thinking is the role of the stress response; it makes us impulsive. However, if we take the time to reflect and respond, we are likely to make a more rational decision. We also have the option to call on more resources or people to support us by using our tend-and-befriend connection energy to problem solve.

The Power of Words

We have already mentioned the power of words in the context of stress energy and it is equally important now we're talking about triggers. The English language is rich, descriptive and plentiful, yet we repeat the word 'stress' as a one-size-fits-all word. Doing this does not help us to define our triggers or the level of threat they represent. Try to make your descriptions specific and convey what you really mean.

Take a moment to consider how many times you've described yourself as 'feeling stressed' recently. It's incredibly common to slip the word 'stress' into any conversation to describe feelings of mild worry or discomfort. Misuse and exaggeration in itself may be a further trigger for our emotional stress response.

EXERCISE: Develop a Wider Emotional Vocabulary

Get friendly with your dictionary and thesaurus and come up with more expressive subtle descriptions of your triggers and how you feel.

- As an example, here are some alternatives to 'stressed': annoyed, frightened, afraid, pressured, frustrated, irritated, confused, worried, upset, peeved, flustered, challenged, uncomfortable, uneasy, tense, disappointed, hurt, lost, trapped, ticked off, impatient, alarmed, trembly, shaken, disturbed, horrified.
- Try this for yourself. Choose another word that has a general meaning – angry, sad, or unhappy will do for now – and see how many alternative expressions you can find.

We have a wonderful language, let's use it to help us navigate stress.

Conditioning and Negative Self-talk Patterns

Animals and humans can be trained to make an automatic association between two events that occur at the same time.

The scientist Ivan Petrovich Pavlov did experiments with dogs in which he rang a bell when he served their food, which made them salivate. Eventually, the dogs salivated on hearing the bell, regardless of whether food was present or not. it's just possible that repeated use of the word 'stress' may be conditioning you to feel fearful and anxious even when you are not under threat.

How we talk to ourself when no one is looking can make us feel stressed. These negative patterns create cognitive distortions, a biased way of seeing things and looking at the world, and because we repeat them unconsciously they can be an invisible trigger for stress. We need to get into the habit of being kinder to ourselves so that we don't allow these negative patterns to set off a stress reaction.

Negative self-talk as a stressor can take a variety of forms, here are a few.

- **Extreme thinking (generalizing):** If I have one drink tonight I will get drunk and make a fool of myself; I burnt the roast potatoes so Sunday lunch is a disaster; my car has started rattling, the engine's going to explode.
- **Black and white thinking (all or nothing, this or that):** I only had five hours' sleep – I must get a solid eight hours to avoid insomnia; there's no point carrying on with this project, we don't have yellow highlighters.
- **Predictive thinking and mind reading (jumping to conclusions):** My boyfriend is late – he must be cheating on me; I know you are going to hate this present I bought you; if we get on that flight it's going to be a big mistake; I've got a feeling in my bones that something bad is going to happen; they've started whispering, I bet they're talking about me.

- **Catastrophising (magnifying and exaggerating):** If I get this presentation wrong I am going to lose my job and then I'll lose my flat; my heart's beating really fast, I think I'm going to have a heart attack.
- **Disqualifying the positives (mental filtering):** She told me I was smart but she doesn't know what I'm really like; they said they enjoyed my singing but they were only being kind.
- **Critical judgemental thinking (self-labelling):** I spilt my drink again – I am such an idiot; I forgot to put the bins out – I'm losing my mind; I'm such a loser for sending a text message with mistakes; my supervisor gave me her pile of work and I smiled – I'm so weak.
- **Perfectionism and procrastination:** I must check those statistics one more time, it looks wrong; I ought to get this right, I have a physics degree; I should be able to do 100 press ups at the gym by now.
- **Taking things personally (or blaming others):** I forgot to send a birthday card – that's why mum sounded annoyed at me; we all had to work late today because I messed up the appointment system.

EXERCISE: Thought Patterns that Can Lead to Stress

The above groups of thought patterns can contribute to feelings of stress – do any apply to you?

- Go through the list above and write in your notebook any of the negative self-talk patterns you recognize.
- Write in your own statements to develop how you feel.
- Can you think of ways to change those negative thoughts? Write some statements to counter the negative ones you have written.

Automatic reactions are difficult to wrangle with so take it slowly and don't be hard on yourself. It will take time to get rid of these negative thoughts, but remember the process of neuroplasticity breaks and changes habits.

Core Beliefs and Rules

Another set of potential triggers is found in our core beliefs. These stem from our upbringing and social settings and can be so ingrained that we treat them like inflexible rules. Young children, subjected to the core beliefs inherited from their parents and those around them, believe the judgements that adults make about them. Until we develop the cognitive ability to question the truth, our perceptions about ourselves and others are shaped by parents, caregivers, teachers and others of influence.

We endeavour to live up to these beliefs, but when we can't we make up additional rules to hide our presumed imperfections from the world – thereby creating more 'unrealistic' core beliefs and stories about ourselves.

Core beliefs and rules can be unrealistically high, but we have an opportunity to question these childhood standards in adulthood. Many are easy to spot from the language we use, such as 'I ought to do this', 'I must remember to do that', 'I should be able to do this'.

One of My Personal Core Beliefs

I always thought: 'I must be smart at all times.' It's an impossible request and it forced me to behave in odd ways to prevent people seeing my believed imperfections and my real fear that I was actually stupid. I worked extra hard at school, did overtime at work, scanned news reports and journals to stay up to date on trends, retrained and got more qualifications than I needed! It was exhausting and stressful. With hindsight, I'd have done things differently.

Childhood

Childhood experiences lay the foundation for how sensitive we are to change, chaos and crisis. It sets our resilience and stress tolerance levels. It establishes our core beliefs and can be the source of adult stressors.

A child who grows up in a chaotic home with parents who argue loudly, or even violently, and have substance abuse issues will have a different set of stress triggers than a child who grows up in a calmer household where parents are reliable and loving, and talk through problems rather than resort to yelling, alcohol or drugs. The first child is likely to have more extreme stress reactions because they learned to manage the chaos by staying vigilant and on the lookout for trouble, which can make them an anxious child and an anxious adult.

Parenting has a big impact on how children learn to deal with stress and anxiety as well as difficult emotions. Good parenting acts as an emotional buffer for young children. When a child gets frustrated or angry, they can turn to a caregiver who comforts, calms and soothe them, plus the caregiver teaches them how to handle complex emotions in the future. A child needs to know they are loved and cared for above all else.

Childhood can also be a source of hugely positive memories that you can draw on to build and maintain a positive outlook.

EXERCISE: Childhood Patterns

Think about any emotional and mental patterns you learned during childhood and analyse them to assess how well they helped you meet your needs as an adult.

- Think of one negative pattern that has been with you since childhood. For example, do you start an argument if you and your partner disagree because that's what your parents used to do?
- Apply the TEA Cycle to the scenario to assess the thoughts, feelings and action you associate with that situation, then rework it again taking a more positive path.
- Now think of one positive pattern from your childhood. Which parent instilled this way of dealing with things in you? How do you repeat the pattern in your life?

Try to deal with behaviour patterns as ghosts from the past that can lead to instability, dependency or aggression.

Ongoing Low-impact Stressors

We tend to associate stressors with circumstances or events that are one-offs or major traumas, but minor annoyances can also lead to stress if they continue relentlessly for a period of time. A dripping tap is no big deal, but imagine being forced to listen to it drip-drip-dripping, hour upon hour – it's possible to suffer from low-level stress in a similar fashion. An accumulation of small stressors can create chronic long-term stress issues and impact wellbeing. Here's a selection for you to consider:

- **Social circumstances:** Are you constantly concerned about poor accommodation, fear of poverty, lack of food, a noisy or dangerous neighbourhood or gang violence?
- **Prejudice:** Do you live with intense and constant prejudice, racism and discrimination, perhaps because you come from a minority group?
- **Financial strain:** Are you just about making ends meet but cannot relax for a moment because your finances are so unstable?
- **Medical issues:** Do you have to cope with a chronic or painful health condition that means activities are curtailed in one way or another?
- **Irrational fears and phobias:** Do you suffer from any phobias or Irrational fears, such as flying, speaking to strangers, public speaking, heights?
- **Childhood attitudes and beliefs:** Are you maintaining out-of-date belief systems?

EXERCISE: Identifying Low-impact Stressors

Can you identify any low-lying stress triggers in your life?

- How do you feel you are affected by this low-level stress? Work out the specific times at which you react negatively to this stressor. Does a gradual build-up of stress result in an occasional reaction?
- How does the TEA Cycle help? Can you think of ways to change your perception? How can you think about

it in a different way? What would be the impact of that change on your emotions and actions?

- Implement the TEA Cycle to find other ways to deal with the problem.
- Working backwards, create a step-by-step schedule or plan to solve the situation.

Remember, you need to define the problem, release the stress energy and redirect it into challenge energy or connection, then take action.

Internal Fear Stressors

These emotions can be the result of thoughts or front-line stressors that activate our threat response. The situations can be real or imagined but feel life-threatening. There are no 'good' or 'bad' emotions, only signals and supporting information about our environment.

- **Anger:** Anger makes us protect something we value and fear losing. It protects our personal space and boundaries when we feel invaded or under attack. It gives us the energy to fight.
- **Fear:** Feeling afraid of situations with the potential to be physically mentally or emotionally damaging. It triggers the fight-or-flight stress response.

- **Worry:** Also called rumination, worry is a chronic emotion in response to a real or imagined situation that troubles us; we repeatedly turn over solutions in our mind, trying to find a resolution.
- **Concern:** A less intense emotion that draws our attention to potential situations worthy of keeping an eye on.
- **Doubt and 'what if':** The 'what if' question pretends to be helpful but destroys confidence about the next action step. It points out flaws, mistakes and makes us second guess things will go wrong. It stops progress.
- **Anxiety:** This is not an illness – it's an emotional reaction to the stress response. However, long-term presence creates a series of illnesses called anxiety disorders. Fear of uncertainty in the future creates the desire for certainty in the now; we become hyper-vigilant (twitchy), overestimate danger, underestimate our ability to cope, and it's exhausting.
- **Panic:** This is an extreme form of anxiety. Godzilla on the rampage! Fearful thoughts escalate in the mind and uncomfortable physiological symptoms create an intense and overwhelming feedback loop. Negative thoughts and symptoms (wrongly) provide evidence that something is wrong, which triggers even more symptoms and negative thoughts. We have already touched on breathing techniques (page 54) and the TEA Cycle to help with symptoms and we will look at other options in chapter 6.

EXERCISE: Stress and Fear-based Emotions

Can you think of a time when any of the fear-based emotions listed on pages 105–106 have been a trigger for your stress?

- Write down the circumstances in which an emotion tripped your stress response.
- What were the circumstances and the resulting emotion?
- Which words would you use to describe how you felt?
- Now think of positive words that would resolve those emotional feelings.

The simple act of identifying the emotions we experience can break negative loops and get our logic to calm things down. Create some distance by saying 'I notice anger' or 'I notice anxiety' instead of stating 'I am angry' or 'I am anxious' – this helps you take charge and take back control of emotions, rather than the emotions taking control of you.

Negative and Positive Stressors

Most of the triggers we have been talking about have been negative stressors, which need to be assessed and re-evaluated so that we can deal with them appropriately.

But there are plenty of positive life stressors, events that certainly put us under pressure but skip past the threat phase straight to the challenge energy phase. New challenges and changes in our lives may raise our stress levels and give us the feeling that we are stepping into the unknown, but we are fully prepared to face the challenges because we are fired up by useful positive energy.

If you can't find any positive stressors, try looking harder and in more detail. Have a go at the exercise opposite. Even if you can only find the smallest particle of positivity, it will be there.

Positive triggers can come under any of the same five important broad areas of your life that we defined earlier.

- **Environment:** Moving home, going on holiday, creating a garden, a community initiative, supporting local charities, learning a new hobby, skill or activity.
- **Relationships:** Embarking on a new relationship or leaving an unsatisfactory one, getting married, having a child, getting a pet, meeting long-lost friends, getting to know yourself better.
- **Work:** New job, promotion, winning an award, relocation to your dream city, resolving a dispute, retiring.
- **Money:** Getting a raise or a better-paid job, making money from a hobby or skill, downsizing your home, starting a savings scheme, learning how to budget.

- **Health:** Recovering from an illness, undergoing a successful surgery, starting a healthy eating plan or exercise routine, running a marathon, working with a doctor or holistic therapist to maintain health.

EXERCISE: Your Positive Stressors

Here are some positive emotional states to aim for: loved, joyful, contented, happy, cheerful, satisfied, delighted, thankful, serene, curious, excited, peaceful, proud, amused, inspired, calm, awed, motivated.

Use your positive stressors as a blueprint for bringing more energy into your life.

- Make a list of the positive stressors in your life. Choose one to focus on.
- If you really are at a point where you cannot identify any positives, use your imagination. What would you most like to have to cope with? Perhaps moving to a new home or getting promoted at work.
- Choose half a dozen things that you would need to do to make sure the new energising event went smoothly. Think of them in terms of the challenge they represent and how you will find the attitude and skills to rise to it.

Seek a balanced life to counteract the inevitable negative stressors. Remind yourself to be just as much on the look-out for positive stressors and emotional states – I call these 'the antidote' — and recognize, enjoy and value the energy boost they can provide.

EXERCISE: Building Your Stress Toolkit

Having looked in detail at the triggers of your stress, make a list of the stress triggers that are currently active in your life. You can use the headings in this book as a guide, but you can be specific to your life experiences and go into as much detail as you like. The more aware and tuned-in you are to your own circumstances the better. Make sure you give specific examples. Now answer the following questions in your notebook.

- Which issues affect you the most? Rank them in order of priority.
- What thoughts do these stressors set in train? Write down your instinctive reactions.
- What kind of energy do they give out? Are they positive stressors emitting high-frequency energy to lift you up and help you rise to the challenge? Or are they negative stressors feeding your fear energy that pulls you down?
- What were your main thoughts associated with each one? How could you change those thoughts?

- What were your main emotions associated with each one? What is the impact of your alternative thoughts?
- How did you behave in response to those thoughts and emotions? How would you behave in the same circumstances in future?

This should give you a comprehensive picture of where your problem areas are and the techniques you can use to break away from negative energy and move towards a positive outcome.

Writing things down will clarify things in your mind and help you to get the best out of the information and data you gather. From now on, be more consciously aware of your triggers; notice when and where you are when they occur and keep notes. In chapter 5, we will look at more strategies to deal with how you are feeling.

Stress Energy Assessment

Now you have read this chapter, rerun your Stress Energy Assessments (pages 14–15), applying your new understanding, and fill in your progress graph.

5

HOW DO YOU EXPERIENCE STRESS?

We are all beautifully and uniquely different. No two people will handle a stress-inducing situation in the same way due to their upbringing and different life experiences. When we feel stressed, we can experience a variety of negative thoughts, uncomfortable emotions and physiological sensations. Emotions can feel too big to handle. Physical sensations can feel overwhelming. We know that the body and mind are intricately connected, and in this chapter we will work out how exactly you experience this.

Physiological Effects of Stressors

Our body is aware of danger even before we register it consciously and releases hormones that turn certain systems on or off. The physical changes that you might experience when your stress response is triggered can be disconcerting until you understand why they happen. There is no particular sequence, but one response can have a knock-on effect on others. We now know this is the body's way of keeping us safe.

- **Immediate physical symptoms:** These might include feeling tense, hot and sweaty, headaches or migraines, rapid breathing, rapid heartbeat, unsettled stomach.
- **Longer-term symptoms:** If you do not deal constructively with your stress, longer-term physical symptoms can be more extreme. These include exhaustion and burnout, headaches and migraines, brain fog, hair loss,

gastrointestinal issues, low immune system (so subject to colds and minor ailments, skin irritation and insomnia).

In all cases, there is a reason for these responses, all related to setting you up to cope with a perceived threat or indicating the presence of unresolved chronic stress.

- **Brain:** Sudden changes to serotonin in the brain constricts blood vessels or releases neuropeptides, causing us to feel lightheaded or the start of a headache or migraine.
- **Digestive system:** The production of digestive enzymes decreases so you may experience butterflies, churning, cramps or vomiting. Your appetite may increase or decrease. An increase in stomach acid can lead to heartburn. A slowing of movement of food through the intestines can cause constipation, diarrhoea or nausea.
- **Eyes:** Pupils dilate, giving tunnel vision as the muscles in the eye contract as we try to focus on distant objects and let in more light. This can create blurred vision or an ache.
- **Heart:** The heart races and the blood vessels constrict to push oxygenated blood to the muscles and brain creating high blood pressure; chronic stress can eventually damage blood vessels.
- **Lungs:** Our breathing becomes shallow and fast as our chest muscles tense to take in more oxygen and pump it to the brain and large muscle groups. This can result in a dry throat and mouth, and can cause dizziness and hyperventilation as the carbon dioxide to oxygen balance is altered (we fail to release enough carbon dioxide).
- **Muscles:** Muscles tense, preparing for quick action, so they can shake and tremble and lead to aches, pains or

backache. These aches and pains can further disrupt sleep patterns. Constriction of the bladder muscles may give you the urge to urinate. Tightening of the jaw muscles may make you clench your teeth.

- **Sleep:** A decrease in the hormone melatonin makes it harder to fall asleep. Regular lack of sleep increases the production of cortisol, which can disrupt sleep patterns further.

- **Skin:** The blood vessels in the skin constrict, the skin pales, the hair stands on end. You might sweat to cool the body. Hands, in particular, can get cold as vessels constrict and pump blood to major muscles. Sometimes the skin can feel itchy, or stress can cause a flare up of skin problems or rashes, such as psoriasis, eczema, rosacea or hives.

- **Immune system:** The body's protective mechanism is weakened, making you more subject to infection.

EXERCISE: Your Personal Physiological Responses

Create a list of the physical symptoms and sensations in your notebook that you experience as a result of stress and analyse them so you can recognize the early signs.

- What are the first physical symptoms you experience when exposed to your stress triggers?
- How quickly do you recognize these symptoms?

- What can you do to stop them? Does deep breathing, for example, help to calm you?
- What happens if you cannot ease the symptoms?
- What happens if you can relieve the symptoms?

This exercise will help you stay alert to your physical responses and try to deal with them to minimize the effects of your stress.

The Hamster Wheel of Rumination

Whatever your stress triggers, you will almost certainly have noticed that when you get stressed you seem to climb on a mental hamster wheel and begin churning things over and over in your mind. Rumination and over-thinking are the mind's way of trying to problem solve, but it soaks up energy and is irritating and painfully overwhelming. It is also like rolling a snowball – it picks up more triggers (problems) as it rolls along. Use the TEA Cycle to break the vicious circle and use your rumination to spot constructive positive outcomes.

The mind can also do the opposite and block out problems. Be bold and address it using your TEA Cycle.

Mental and Emotional Effects of Stress

You may experience psychological reactions to your stress triggers, again designed to help you cope with a threat but not necessarily appropriate to the kind of stressors you are experiencing. Symptoms that affect your mental health are likely to be more related to ongoing stress than an immediate reaction to a stress trigger.

- **Brain:** The thoughts are racing to try to evaluate the level of threat and make critical decisions. That makes it hard to focus thoughts on anything other than the feeling of anxiety and danger. Longer-term, this can lead to anxiety and depression.
- **Reproductive system:** Longer-term disruption to the hormones can disrupt the menstrual cycle, reduce sex drive as testosterone levels drop, and lead to erectile dysfunction or fertility issues.
- **Fatigue:** General tiredness leading, over time, to a feeling of physical and mental exhaustion.

Imagine watching a river fill up with more and more water until it can no longer hold what's there. It bursts its banks and spills over. We too can feel flooded by overwhelming anxious thoughts and emotions. On the other hand, there are times when we can't let the emotion flow, so we keep it all in. We can become so good at holding back that it makes us emotionally numb.

When we experience powerful emotions, the body shuts down the rational-thinking brain. You may notice you can't think straight, you get brain fog or your mind goes blank. The stress response is designed to do this; it wants us to focus on getting away from the danger, not on trying to weigh up dangers, as this would waste precious time and jeopardize our survival.

Post-traumatic Stress Disorder (PTSD)

We usually hear about PTSD in a military context, but it can affect anyone in any age group who has witnessed or been involved in an atrocity or an accident. When we do something repeatedly for long enough it becomes a habit, and that includes harmful patterns of behaviour and thinking. When we add to this process fear, trauma or a terrible life event, the images get stuck in our brain and re-trigger the event. The unprocessed memory creates distressing flashbacks and nightmares long after the danger has passed, triggering the most extreme of stress responses. Professional help is required to deal with such extreme experiences of stress.

Note that sometimes you are perfectly capable of handling a situation, but that same problem at a different point in time seems impossible to cope with. Instead of being tough on yourself, check if this is because of any changes in your physical, emotional or mental wellbeing (hunger, thirst, loneliness, illness, tiredness, lack of fresh air, sudden issues at home or work).

It can help to look for patterns in our stress responses and that is why your notebook is so important. This might be a good time to look back through your notebook and see how many of your entries relate to an emotional response to a stress trigger.

EXERCISE: Looking for Patterns in Emotional Stress Triggers

Make another note in your notebook that records where you are in relation to emotional responses.

- How many times have you recorded an emotional response?
- Can you see a pattern emerging that allows you to define the TEA Cycle associated with this emotion?

Allow yourself to examine both of these responses and find a pattern to add to your overall stress and TEA Cycle landscape. Spotting patterns helps us create a strategy to prevent old behaviours bubbling up in the future, and gives us the opportunity to find alternative ways of thinking, feeling and behaving.

Why We Need an Emotional Response

Have you ever wondered why we have emotions when they can involve pain and distress? There are many theories, but they all agree that – quite apart from the fact that they can bring us such joy – emotions are useful messengers prompting some form of action. They tell us a lot about our internal and external environment – our levels of danger or safety, sadness or happiness, connection or isolation. Expanding our emotional vocabulary helps us clearly identify the message and see how it fits into the TEA Cycle, which helps us deconstruct / reconstruct stressors and change them, as well as improving our communication with others.

In 1980, psychologist Robert Plutchik suggested that emotions had evolved to push us towards certain social advantages and interactions.[14]

- **Affiliation:** Acceptance and trust help us to connect with others and groups.
- **Protection:** Fear leads to retreat and withdrawal from something harmful.
- **Exploration:** Curiosity and play help us investigate our environment.
- **Orientation:** Surprise helps us react and respond to new things.
- **Rejection:** Disgust helps us to get rid of things that are harmful.
- **Destruction:** Anger leads to getting rid of barriers stopping us get what we need.
- **Incorporation:** Acceptance helps us absorb things that are good for us.

- **Reintegration:** Sadness and grief help us recognize we've lost something of value and carry on.
- **Reproduction:** Joy and pleasure help us bond, mate and keep the species going.

EXERCISE: Encouraging Your Emotions

Can you think of a time when your emotions have helped you take positive action?

- Look at the list above and write down the emotions you feel the most and those you would like to feel more of.
- Think about the impact of introducing them into the TEA Cycle. What positive thoughts might give rise to those emotions and what actions might be the result?
- Congratulate yourself on generating something good from a negative emotional state.

Repetitive Impact Response

Events, people or places influence our opinions, expectations, assumptions, rules and beliefs. When the same thought is constantly repeated, it strengthens our conviction that it is fact rather than opinion. Hanging on to outmoded opinions is another way we can experience – and perpetuate – stress.

The brain is lazy! It doesn't waste energy reassessing familiar behaviours, nor reassessing the thoughts stored about ourselves (self-esteem) or of other people (judgements). The brain creates templates of behavioural and thinking habits and sets them on autopilot. The problem is that some of these past behaviours or opinions may no longer be true or in our best interests, but the data has not been updated. When faced with a trigger, it sparks off that harmful and out-of-date thought and a negative TEA Cycle is set in motion. Therefore, it's essential to examine thinking patterns and habits by questioning, challenging and interrogation.

Negative Self-talk Traps

We have already looked at how negative self-talk can be a stressor in itself because thoughts come automatically into our brains and set off a stress response. The same negative self-talk can also be a result of a specific thinking pattern and so exacerbate the problem.

Human beings may be warriors but, unfortunately, we are also excellent worriers. We are meaning-making machines that worry about things that happened in the past, and worry about things that might happen in future. Memories come as a package deal, the thought plus the emotions we felt at that time. If used creatively and positively, that can be good – this powerful gift is at the heart of our creativity. But when this superpower is used in the wrong way, the imagined horror story creates anxiety. If we create anxiety while daydreaming imaginatively, we will experience our stress response in the present moment. Have a look at the thinking traps we can fall into during negative self-talk below. It's like forgetting we are wearing a pair of dark sunglasses.

Extreme thinking

When we have extreme thoughts, we make generalized statements without enough evidence, glossing over any information we simply don't like or that doesn't fit in with the way we see ourselves or other people. Distorting and filtering information forces it to fit in with our life experiences and world view, but this can only happen by cheating or lying to ourselves.

Black and white thinking

Sometimes we only see the extreme options: either I'm safe or I'm in danger; either there is food to eat or no food. It's quite an easy way of thinking to fall into because having only two outcomes takes a lot of the worry and anxiety out of decision-making. Sometimes this way of thinking is essential, for example: is it safe to cross the road or not? But often there are more choices, shades of grey, and perhaps neither extreme option is the right one.

Predictive thinking

Imagine a bear or lion comes past our cave every evening at 7pm and takes whichever child is playing outside the cave. Eventually, we would predict this distressing daily event and stop the children playing outside during this critical moment.

Fast forward to today, and we are forever guessing, jumping to conclusions, thinking that we know what somebody else is about to say or think, but we don't have the gift of clairvoyance. We play an emotionally charged guessing game with no concrete facts or evidence, just a series of assumptions, guesses and opinions. The worst thing about predictive thinking is that we often focus on negative outcomes without considering positive ones. Our thoughts are out of balance and exaggerated. We don't spend all day thinking about inheriting a fortune, being given a rise at work, or finding a partner who loves and adores us. Instead, we spend valuable time catastrophizing and seeing the sinking of the *Titanic* round every corner.

Dark and gloomy outlook

Predictive thinking leads to a gloomy view of the world, and we can feel nervous, on-edge and dread things going wrong. The belief that events are not going to work out well can seep into every area of life. Problems feel permanent and personal. We fail to see the successes and only notice the failures, yet somehow we spot everyone else's successes and ignore their failures. We blame ourselves for creating negative situations.

Filtering out the good stuff

We become our own worst enemy if we think in this way: a self-critical punisher who minimizes the good stuff and exaggerates the bad. We compare ourselves to others and despair. We downplay our achievements, skills talents and good points and upgrade everyone else's. We find it hard to say complimentary things about ourselves and fail to celebrate wins or successes.

Critical judgemental thinking

I hate being criticized! You can dress it up as feedback or another word, but I still end up feeling hurt and a failure. However, it wasn't always like that. Children are not born with the fear of not being good enough. They simply learn the risk of verbal assault or abandonment, and learn the rewards of obedience and compliance to those with power. When we receive a lot of negative feedback about what we do, the way we behave or how we look during childhood and our teen years, this drives 'not good enough' thoughts.

Some of us struggle to get back into other people's good books and try to live up to the pressure of their unrealistic expectations, hopes or dreams. We all do this people-pleasing to some degree to receive the praise, love and care that humans need. We remain vulnerable and crave reassurance, but this is a burdensome way to live. As adults, we need to remind ourselves that we don't need to keep trying to impress people, nor do we have to be in their good books. Just do your best (this is good enough). It generates a huge feeling of relief and satisfaction. It stops us demanding perfection in everything we do. Even in nature the imperfect things are 'perfect.'

I take the pressure off myself by reciting, 'I am perfectly imperfect or imperfectly perfect'.

Perfectionism and procrastination

We set high unrealistic standards and fear failure. We demand this of ourselves and others. Some of this behaviour harks back to the past and some come from our role models – family members, school, celebrities and other influencers. Unrealistic standards ironically set us up for failure. We procrastinate, put things off, try to get every small detail right before starting or finishing projects. This strategy essentially attempts to avoid future embarrassment, humiliation or failure. The biggest downside? We avoid learning or trying new activities, expanding our skillset or simply having fun.

EXERCISE: Harmful Thinking Traps

Which of the above thinking traps do you fall into?

- Choose one or two of the harmful thinking patterns that you are prone to when you are stressed.
- Try to listen to yourself when you are talking (as though you were a fly on the wall) and see if you can catch yourself falling into these traps.

• Write your own experience of what triggers the thinking and how you feel about it.

Stopping yourself from the invasion of ANTs (automatic negative thoughts) is part of taking back control of your rational thinking and dampening the irrational ones.

Negative Assumptions

We have many ideas and opinions, and make major assumptions but treat them as if they were facts. Our negative assumptions can become core beliefs, the things we believe to 'be true' about ourselves. This way of thinking is flawed and makes stress symptoms more severe. Here's a selection of some broad categories of harmful core beliefs we keep hidden from the world.

I Am Unlovable

We believe we don't belong or are undeserving of love. It leads to feelings of loneliness and superficial relationships to avoid the pain of rejection.

Other ways of expressing this negative: I am not wanted; I am unacceptable; I am unattractive; I don't fit in; I don't matter to anyone; I am bound to be rejected; I'm not interesting.

I Must Be Responsible

We believe we must sacrifice our own needs, and feel guilty when we don't. We have to keep others happy, and may have played this role in our family.

Other ways of expressing this negative: My needs are not important; if I care enough, I can fix them; I have to do things by myself; if I make a mistake I'm a failure; I must do everything perfectly; I mustn't ask for help; if I don't do it then nobody else will; people can't be trusted to look after themselves.

I Will Be Abandoned

We fear losing anyone we get close to and believe that when we do get close they will ultimately leave us. We seek lots of reassurance and don't speak up for ourselves so as not to upset others.

Other ways of expressing this negative: People will leave me; if I care for someone I will be abandoned; if I speak up for myself people will leave me; I am bound to be abandoned; I am not important.

I Am Helpless and Powerless

We believe we have no control and can't handle things independently, or we go to the other extreme and are over-controlling or manipulative.

Other ways of expressing this negative: I am weak; I am vulnerable; I can't stand up for myself or say no; I am trapped; I can't achieve anything; I am needy.

I Am Inferior

We believe we are flawed or incompetent or stupid, and that sooner or later others will discover this. It is the basis of 'imposter' syndrome.

Other ways of expressing this negative: There's something wrong with me; I am not good enough: I am abnormal; I've done something wrong; I never get things right; I am stupid and useless; I am a failure; I am a bad person; I am worthless; I am insignificant.

I Am Special and Entitled To Things

We make demands, feel we are superior and deserve attention and praise, perhaps overcompensating for the fact we feel inferior and unwanted. We break rules and are jealous of other people's success.

Other ways of expressing this negative: I am entitled to special treatment; if I don't do well I am inferior and worthless; people have no right to criticize me; I am not bound by the rules of others.

EXERCISE: Defining Your Negative Thoughts

Dwelling on negativity is bad for mental, emotional and physical health, so choose just one of the negative thoughts listed above that could apply to you. Apply your TEA Cycle thinking.

- Write down the main thought in your notebook.
- Populate it with statements that you have made or thought.
- How else could you have responded?

Work mindfully when examining negative thoughts. They touch on sensitive areas that feel uncomfortable and may bring back childhood memories – don't dwell too long. Move on to positive ways of reframing thoughts through the eyes of the 'adult' you.

EXERCISE: Building Your Stress Response Picture

Your stress response picture is building up and now you can add more information to it. In your notebook:

- Create a list of the physical reactions you experience to stress.
- Create a list of your psychological and emotional reactions.
- Include negative thinking patterns or any other stressors from this chapter.
- Identify them as internal or external.
- Mark them as positive or negative.

Retake the baseline figures, lifestyle questionnaire and update your weekly or monthly Stress Energy Assessment graph (from page 17). How does your SEA compare now with how it was at the beginning of the book?

Moving Forward

The ways we experience stress are broad and unique to us, influenced by our innate nature, moulded by our childhood and our past, and infinitely variable depending on the circumstances in which we find ourselves. When we get caught up in negative feelings it can be triggered by memories from the past, and outdated automatic internal responses and mental instructions float to the surface of our mind.

Knowing what is happening in our bodies and our minds, however, is a huge step forward in creating our unique map to navigate our way through stress. In the next chapter we will move on to the all-important ways of dealing with our stress and living our lives free of the negative pressures of stress.

Stress Energy Assessment

Now you have read this chapter, rerun your Stress Energy Assessments (pages 14–15), applying your new understanding, and fill in your progress graph.

6

WHAT CAN YOU DO ABOUT STRESS?

It's time to explore some strategies and tools that will help us navigate our stress, embracing the positive, finding immediate responses to short-term stress and deeper options to deal with the long-term impact of repeatedly hitting the stress button or, even worse, leaving it permanently in the 'on' position.

TEA Cycle Training

First of all, remind yourself that you can use your TEA Cycle training to deconstruct any stressful situation, and I encourage you to use it regularly. Go back to pages 51–57 to remind yourself how it works. The more you examine the way you react to stress, the easier it will become to construct positive scenarios to replace the negative ones. Soon it will become second nature and then you are halfway to beating your stress – all the way will be when you do it so automatically that you no longer need it. Do remember, though, that there are no right or wrong answers.

EXERCISE: Building Your TEA Muscle Memory

Here's a reminder of how the TEA Cycle helps you look for alternatives to your stressful reactions using a deconstruction and reconstruction of your thoughts, emotions and actions.

- Write down your Thoughts, Emotions and Actions in relation to a particular circumstance.
- Think about the consequences of each one.
- Challenge your thinking and replace your initial thoughts, then interrogate what happens to the emotions and actions.

You can do this as often as you like to as many situations as you need. Look for a positive outcome.

By definition, the TEA Cycle works in every direction. Just change one of the elements and see what the consequences are. Change thoughts, and see what happens to emotions and actions. Change emotions and see what happens to actions and thoughts. Change actions and see what happens to thoughts and emotions.

Controlling the Stress Response

The body has a clever way of rebalancing itself called homeostasis – returning to standby mode. When it gets the message that the danger is over – when our breathing slows down and is back to normal, our thoughts are no longer racing and we feel calm and safe – then it turns on the relaxation response and switches off the stress hormones. So, by learning to understand what is happening and why – which hopefully you have understood from the earlier chapters – you will be able to recognize and assess your triggers and change your response to stress. Knowledge is power, and that can be as good as hitting the off button to calm the body and return to standby mode. Keep practising your TEA Cycle.

Using Stress Energy

Another skill we have already covered is using and controlling your stress energy. Go back to Chapter 3 to remind yourself how it works. Fear and threat are low-frequency energies that lower performance. Challenge energy involves higher frequency emotions – such as excitement, curiosity and motivation – and can lead to higher performance, greater accuracy and alertness, and better co-ordination and focus.

When your threat response is activated, you feel a rush of stress energy. How do you change that to the challenge energy that is going to help you? The transformation of energy is only achieved by recognizing that you are no longer under threat and can return to normal functioning, at which point the hormones that have been rushing around your system ringing alarm bells will be rebalanced, leaving the energy to be redirected. That process can be learned by practising your TEA Cycle and applying it to the stressful circumstances you encounter.

EXERCISE: Using Role Play to Activate Your Challenge Energy

Focus on this example or make up your own, applying the TEA Cycle to make yourself aware of the changing energy.

- You are going to a conference; this is not in your comfort zone and has sparked a negative stress response.
- Imagine you are someone else – visualize a colleague, a friend or a celebrity. You've stepped into their shoes, what would they be thinking? It would not be fear. But it might be confidence, excitement, enthusiasm.
- Sit quietly and imagine that you are them, thinking their thoughts. Really try and get under their skin and feel the way they do.
- Work from thoughts to feelings to actions and visualize the event.
- Gradually move back to reality, put yourself back in the picture, but hang on to the positive thoughts and insights that will help you rise to the challenge.

Don't assume that nobody else feels nervous or apprehensive – they do! These feelings add fuel to the challenge energy that will help you do a good job.

The third level of energy is connection energy, or tend and befriend, which allows you to reach out to seek or offer resources, care and support to those around you.

Coping with Lifestyle Stressors

Forewarned is forearmed – so the old saying goes. The most straightforward thing you can do in the short term to avoid stress, is to avoid your stress triggers. However, this can make anxieties worse not better and create phobias, because stressors are part of the fabric of life and some are unavoidable. We will be looking at a variety of ways to deal with them as we go through this chapter. Remember: life is unpredictable and full of uncertainty and surprises, but humans are well equipped to deal with short-term stress. So get used to stretching your coping skill muscles. Learn to experience uncomfortable stress symptoms for longer periods of time, knowing that they won't kill you – it's just uncomfortable. You build healthier neural pathways (neuroplasticity) by facing real or imagined fears, you can reframe them and realize they are not as bad as you thought.

For example, you are getting stressed about trying to find a new job. Stop. Ask yourself: do you really need to change your job now? Can you put that on hold while you work on building your confidence? Or, you find it difficult to visit a particular restaurant where you broke up with a partner. Stop. Do a bit of internet research to find some more places to go until you can face going there, so when someone says 'Let's go to the Sad Café', you can suggest other venues that you really want to try.

EXERCISE: Avoiding Your Stressors

There will be stress triggers you can avoid in the short term.

- Look through your list of stressors and identify any that you can avoid. Ignore the rest for now.
- Take one at a time and apply your creative imagination to finding alternatives and ways of avoiding them.
- Put your knowledge into practice.

This will stop the stress before it even gets going, so is always the option to try first.

Helping You to Relax

Being stressed can leave you feeling wound up like a clock spring, and releasing that physical tension can be a first step towards coping with the fundamental causes of stress. Here are some tried-and-tested remedies for calming you down mentally and physically.

Hot baths: Especially if you add some luxurious bubbles, scented candles and soft towels, you can really pamper yourself. I prefer Epsom Salts – they contain magnesium which relieves tension and pain, relaxes muscles and promotes sleep.

Head and neck massage: Relaxing muscles around the skull can relieve headaches.

Engage your senses: Nibble a tiny square of exotic chocolate (perhaps while you are in that scented bath), burn incense or fragrant candles, smell essential oils (lavender, lemon), have a massage or gently stimulate any or all of your senses.

Fresh air: Go for a walk or even just sit on the balcony or pop to the corner shop. Get outside and breathe in fresh air, it sends more oxygen to the brain which can affect production of your happy hormone serotonin, and can also help with melatonin and your body clock to promote good sleep.

Exercise: Anything from a run to a yoga class or half a dozen star jumps. Movement is the key word, whatever your level of physical ability.

Hit a punchbag: If you don't happen to have a punchbag available, punch a cushion – get rid of any aggressive energy.

Burn your thoughts: Write down the details of a painful encounter, then safely burn the paper, or scrunch it up or tear it into tiny pieces.

Music: Listen to something calming; there are plenty of soothing music compilations. Depending on how you feel, perhaps go the opposite way, heavy metal or loud music can do the trick.

Lavender: Have you noticed it's the go-to calming herbal fragrance for incense, candles, oils, soap, and putting under your pillow? Or you might have other relaxing favourites, such as ylang ylang.

Get in touch with nature: Get in the garden, the park or, better still, into the countryside and feel your stress melt away on the wind. Nature can reduce blood pressure and calm the nervous system. Eco-therapy research is looking into the benefits of outdoor activities.

Revert to childhood favourites: Do something silly like have a game of hopscotch, or see if you can still skip or do hula hoop. If it's cold enough, build a snowman or have a snowball fight. Pick up a pot of children's bubbles and watch the swirling colours as you blow. Find some colouring pencils and use a colouring-in book.

Meditation: Practise meditation and mindfulness techniques in order to still your mind and relax your body.

EXERCISE: First Meditation

This is just the absolute basics of meditation. Investigate further – there are many useful sites you can access.

- Sit comfortably and start to breathe steadily and deeply, concentrating on filling your lungs.
- Take a deep breath in through the nose and out through the mouth in a steady rhythm.
- As you maintain your breathing, let your muscles relax.
- Close your eyes and let everything go.
- Breathe in the energy; breathe out the tension.
- Pause as you keep the rhythm of your breath. Allow your thoughts to drift where they want to go, don't try to control them.
- Feel totally relaxed and in the moment.
- When you feel ready, slowly open your eyes and bring your focus back to the everyday.

It need only take a few minutes but meditating regularly will help calm your stress levels. Use the body to calm the mind, and vice versa.

Coping with Short-term Physical Symptoms

The physical symptoms of stress are so many and varied that you will need to respond to your own particular physical issues. Remember that this is akin to sticking a plaster over a wound – it might give you the time you need for the wound to heal without you feeling so bad about it. However, you also need to be addressing the problem itself at the same time as coping with the stress reactions in your body.

See Your Doctor

The following are some straightforward ways to deal with immediate physical symptoms to get you through an incident, but they are not intended to replace professional medical help and you should always seek suitable advice if your condition is causing you concern.

There are many ways to cope with headaches: a cold compress, rest, over-the-counter medication, lavender oil on the temples, avoid screen work or close work, such as sewing. Do the same if you find your vision affected. Migraines are more problematic, especially if stress is the trigger rather than a food, for example. Some people find lying down in a darkened room helps if they are able to react quickly enough, but you should speak with your pharmacist or doctor.

If you feel dizzy or light-headed, sit down; the last thing you need is to fall down. If you feel faint and look pale, rest your head on your knees for a few moments. Seek medical advice if this persists as it could be the sign of low blood pressure or an inner ear problem.

If you find your heart beating rapidly or your breathing becoming shallow, the best thing to do is breathe. Please don't dismiss this as simplistic; it really works. Make yourself comfortable, if you can, take a deep breath in through your nose and keep breathing in as long as you can, as though you are trying to fill your lungs and your whole abdomen with air. When you can't breathe in any further, you will automatically breathe out. Keep breathing out as though you want to completely empty your body of air. Do this just two or three times, then let your breathing settle into a natural and deep rhythm.

For those who find their stomach unsettled or feel hot and sweaty, sipping water (not too cold) or peppermint tea should help to calm things down. Spicy or sweet foods are unlikely to help.

Your skin is very sensitive; if stress triggers bring on underlying conditions, such as eczema, you will need to get medical advice on what to do. For minor rashes, your pharmacist should be able to suggest a soothing cream.

Tense muscles can often be relieved by some simple stretching exercises. In fact, a short stretching routine first thing in the morning could set you up for the day. Investigate YouTube for various routines or observe a cat stretching.

Harness the Power of Sleep

Tension in your body can make it difficult to sleep, and if your mind is churning your body will tense – you might even not realize how stressed you are. If you have chronic stress, raised cortisol levels can also disrupt healthy sleep patterns. But getting enough sleep is important as it is the ultimate way to de-stress, repair, recharge and reset your mind and body. How much sleep we need varies, but the traditional eight-hour average is about right, teenagers need more, older people slightly less. When we lose sight of the value of sleep we seriously affect the health of mind and body.

Firstly, did you know that increasing your exposure to daylight can improve your readiness for sleep. Our body's circadian rhythms control internal processes, and the central area of the brain is considered the body's master clock. It operates on roughly a 24-hour sleep-wake cycle and is influenced by light and other cues, such as the time we eat and the amount of exercise we take. Endorphins released by exercising during the day are a great aid to good sleep, but do not exercise too close to bedtime.

Start your good sleep by setting up a favourable environment. Don't have the room too hot or too cold – aim for the Goldilocks temperature! Make sure the room is dark, as light affects melatonin levels that regulate sleep. Have comfortable pillows and a duvet that keeps you warm but not too hot, our temperature needs to dip before falling sleep. Mattresses are a personal choice so find one that suits you. Try to keep your bedroom as somewhere for sex and sleep, if you can – and don't keep a TV, a tablet or a phone in the room – this helps your brain associate the room with sleep.

Have a bedtime routine and stick to it. Wind down, get everything ready for the morning, set your alarm. Some people like a warm milky drink, perhaps with a sprinkling of turmeric. Some people like soothing background music or a recording of a silky voice to listen to (I have heard that Matthew McConaughey has made just such a tape!).

A process of tensing and releasing your muscles called progressive muscle relaxation (PMR) has been scientifically tested and proven to help people get to sleep. Lie comfortably. Pull your toes towards you and spread them apart so that you feel the muscles in your feet; keep them stretched for the count of five, then relax. Tense your calves, hold, then relax. Tense your thighs, hold, then relax. Work your way up your body until finally you screw your face up and tighten your scalp, then relax it. Now that your whole body is relaxed, think peaceful thoughts and hopefully you will drift off to sleep.

EXERCISE: How Well Do You Sleep?

If you are not sleeping well, go through all our sleep advice and personalize it to your needs.

- Check how much exercise and fresh air you get during the day. Perhaps you could add a short walk to your routine. Even small amounts of exposure to sunlight helps the body clock (circadian rhythm).
- Is your bedroom designed for a good sleep? Make some changes if you need to.
- Write down a bedtime routine. We train young children to sleep well because of a wind-down routine.
- Practise the stretch-and-relax sequence for at least a week (PMR, progressive muscle relaxation).

If you see no improvement, go back and try some other options. There are plenty of ideas on YouTube.

Patient Power

Only a generation ago, any doctor who told a patient to 'jump' would receive the response 'how high?' It's an old joke but represents a truth that we have now become more questioning and involved in our healthcare. Patients want to 'play an intelligent, independent and informed role, not merely in terms of decision-making but also in the management of those preventive, diagnostic and therapeutic activities which concern them'.[15] This is sometimes called self-medication. But unless information or products come from a reliable source, this has negative implications.

In a positive way, it can be hugely beneficial to feel you have the power to influence your care and treatment. There are any number of alternative or complementary therapies you can try, from acupuncture to zen therapy. The only important thing is that you keep your medical practitioner informed of what you would like to try so that they can check the treatment is not incompatible with any conventional medical treatment.

Alternative therapies that show anecdotally that they can be of benefit in treating stress include acupuncture and massage therapies, including aromatherapy.

Prescribed Medication

Anxiety and depression can work together like terrible twins. No one knows whether feeling depressed makes you feel more anxious about things, or whether feeling anxious and fearful makes you feel depressed. They both create a sense of hopelessness which can lead to thoughts of self-harm or suicide.

If your anxiety feels out of control and is causing unnecessary distress and stopping you from functioning well at work and in relationships, please seek help. If you had a broken leg or a heart condition you wouldn't just tough it out, would you? No, you'd see a doctor and get some advice or a referral to a specialist health practitioner.

In some cases, you may be prescribed medication to help you get yourself back on track. This helps many people, but if you suspect that medication is adversely affecting your stress response and not helping to ease your depression, look at the contra-indications of your medication and consult your doctor. Never simply stop taking medication, as there can be a negative rebound effect.

If you are taking antidepressant medication in the longer term, there is a risk of addiction as the body adapts, but don't let this scare you off seeking help. Factors such as childhood adversity, childhood lessons learned, personality traits and bad life experiences can make patients more susceptible to addiction. Discuss this with your doctor and they will advise the best course of action. It may be valuable to seek help from a specialist therapist.

Avoiding Negative Influencers

There can be difficulties with taking control of your condition or 'self-medication' that you should be aware of and avoid. As I have said, you should make any decisions in consultation with your doctor so that they can ensure there are no conflicts that would have negative side-effects.

We all know that smoking, drugs and any kind of substance abuse is bad for us. It will only make your stress symptoms worse to continue with those habits. They may feel as though they offer a short-term solution, but they are addictive habits and will contribute to sensations of anxiety, negatively affecting the balance of stress hormones in the body. Plus, they impact the way you feel about yourself, the quality of your personal relationships, finances and work.

Have a look at the major stress-related effects of overindulgence in these behaviours.

Alcohol: Heavy drinking can alter the brain's chemistry, affecting the balance of cortisol and adrenocorticotropic hormone.

Caffeine: Caffeine from coffee or fizzy drinks creates alertness but also a jitteriness and heart palpitations, affecting the stress hormones adrenalin and cortisol.

Smoking: Nicotine stimulates the release of the chemical dopamine in the brain, affecting the body's chemical balance and negatively impacting those experiencing depression.

Gambling: Studies show it releases dopamine in the brain, affecting areas similar to those activated by drug abuse. It can also affect anxiety and problems with both personal relationships and debt, both of which can be stress triggers.

Computer games: Affects dopamine release and can create an addiction. It can also affect anxiety and personal relationships.

Pornography: Can have a similar effect to computer games.

Extreme sports: These can provide an adrenalin rush, but increase the risk of injury or death.

Self-harm: Releases cortisol which acts as a painkiller, but affects the way you manage emotions and could lead to death or serious injury.

Over-exercising: Induces stress on the body, creating excessive pain that releases endorphins and cortisol to give you a 'high'. Can lead to hormonal imbalance including testosterone, drive overeating and burn muscle tissue instead of fat.

Eating disorders: Bulimia, anorexia and other disorders are used to manage tension, stress and unwanted emotions. The body makes serotonin, which boosts your mood, and cortisol, which increases hunger, a desire for sweet foods and carbohydrates. Blood sugar goes up then crashes, making you feel tired, shaky and hungry. This can lead to cycles of bingeing, feeling bad about yourself, bingeing, feeling bad about yourself.

EXERCISE: Check Out Bad Habits

Don't give in – get help and try to give them up!

- Which of the potentially addictive behaviours listed above are part of your life?

- Write down what you get out of the habit.
- Write down the negatives. Include the cost, the opinions of your partner or children, health impacts and anything else.
- What impact does it have on your stress response?
- What will happen if you continue down the same path?
- What will happen if you change?
- Harness those positive reasons for change and write down two or three recommended websites to read, or sources of help and support (see page 211).

You will need the courage to take the first step. Summon all that stress energy you have been wasting and transform it into challenge or connection energy.

An Antidote to Technology

Our technology-dependent, 21st-century lifestyles bombard us with constant notifications that demand our attention. So much so that we are losing our ability to focus and concentrate on one thing, flitting from one task to another, or making endless cups of tea or coffee. Our emails ping, notifications jump up and down like impatient children fighting to grab our attention. We are stalked by wall-to-wall adverts across the internet as we try to read articles. We are almost being programmed to have short attention spans, the knock-on effect being poor concentration, lower productivity and quality of work. Is the technology-biased world we live in the creator of some of your stress? Remember the process of neuroplasticity and how the brain rewires itself because of a repeated experience.

EXERCISE: Being Single-minded Can Reduce Your Stress

Set aside some time to focus on one task in hand.

- Using a scale of 1 to 10, rate your concentration levels and fidgetiness at, say, 10.30am on a normal day (10=high, 1=low)
- Now remove all your weapons of mass distraction (namely your mobile phone). Put your phone out of sight and hearing, or switch it off completely (now there's a novelty!). This will make you feel anxious, you will justify why you cannot do this, you may feel highly resistant to trying this.
- Remove or cover up the notifications panel if you are working on a computer.
- Spend the next 30 minutes focusing on one task to the best of your ability, take a 10-minute break, then repeat.
- Reassess your concentration score at the end of the day. Gather data and try to do this for seven days. Has it improved? Do you feel your headspace is clearer?

Get into the habit of having some time each day when your phone is switched off, or on silent or vibrate mode. You are the master, the phone is your servant (not the other way round).

Changing Your Thought Patterns

Our mind plays a huge role in the stress experience. Many of our stressors are internal, and the stress response is a spiral of unhelpful negative thoughts.

Understanding the connection between what we think, feel and do are critical for successfully managing stress energy. Thoughts have power, and when we think negatively our body is always listening and has the power to dump adrenalin into the blood stream quickly – the stress response. Use the mind to calm the body, or the body to calm the mind.

Positive thinking can become our safety net and a source of building resilience. It sets us up for bearing stress, and creatively using strategies that override negative thinking patterns.

EXERCISE: Thinking Positive

- Start by setting up a self-notification on your phone of the number of times you think negatively, then give yourself a nudge to think positively.
- Start every day with a positive thought or an inspiring word of the day and keep it at the back of your mind. My daily thought is 'be bold'.
- Laugh – tell a joke, watch a TV programme that you find amusing, listen to a comedy show on the radio. Laughing gives you more oxygen and shifts your mood.
- Seek out positive people. We become like the people we surround ourselves with.
- Engage in positive self-talk: say things like 'I look good', 'I can do this', 'I did well' and 'I'll do better next time'. Repeat in your head, out loud or in front of a mirror.

Don't do this just once, make it a habit.

Tricking the Anxious Brain

We have already seen that our hormone systems give off specific responses to external and internal stimuli – certain triggers make us feel stressed – but we can copy the brain's technique and use it against itself. By mimicking specific behaviours that the brain associates with being calm and relaxed, we can trick it into thinking we are calm and relaxed.

We can do this by deep breathing (see page 54) or by progressively relaxing our muscles (see page 148).

We can also trick it by doing activities the brain knows we could not do if we were in a dangerous situation and feeling stressed. For example, the brain knows we would not be able to eat and chew if we were on red alert, running away or fighting. The act of chewing gum (even pretending to chew gum) can trick the brain. Laughing and joking releases the good mood hormone serotonin, this is another behaviour we would not be doing if we were truly fighting for our lives. Have you noticed during tense conversations or situations the mere act of laughing breaks the tension and brings relief?

Laughter is a great stress-buster. Have a joke or two up your sleeve to release the stress, or an image that makes you laugh. The classic actors' example is imagining the audience naked. (Did you hear what one guitar said to the other when he found out he was stressed? 'Hey, man, don't fret!')

Exercise

Exercise can be another way of tricking an anxious brain. Exercise can help you get rid of negative energy and feel more prepared to cope with life's problems – because the body gets accustomed to the symptoms of stress that appear when exercising. The stress response can make you hot, sweaty, out of breath with shaky muscles. Sound familiar? Well, that's what exercise does too. So if your body after exercise knows it's okay to feel like this, it won't be so freaked out if you have a similar response to a trigger. The more often the body experiences the exercise state, the more your brain learns to form new associations. It's hard to believe that doing star jumps or push ups just before an activity that makes you nervous can dampen your fear response, but it does. Fear has an instinctive cycle, the exercise helps it to complete this and discharge the fear-anxiety energy.

So exercise can trick the brain into coping better with the stress response. But exercise – or movement – is good in itself. Exercise keeps joints moving, strengthens muscles and revitalises your brain with oxygen. Imagine your body being a high-performance car, let's say a Ferrari – would you leave it stuck in the garage or would you instinctively know you have to take it for a good run, clear out the cobwebs and hear the engine roar? The mindset shift is to have daily movement as your goal, whatever level of mobility you have.

Aim for Movement over Exercise

There will be some who have read that section with a heavy heart! We know we should all do some daily exercise. If you are a keen keep-fit fan, that's great – just do it. But the problem for some of us with telling ourselves what you 'ought to, should do, must do', is that we rebel and go in the opposite direction. We feel guilty and bad and then turn to some other activity that makes us feel better. Mine is chocolate! I am not a gym bunny, nor do I experience the adrenalin rush with the endorphin hit that some people do when they exercise; I just get hot, sweaty and tired.

However, my brain puts up little resistance to the word 'movement', so my solution is to make sure I keep moving. There's nothing wrong with a walk round the block, a bit of gardening, dancing to the radio, or cleaning the house (well, some people like it!); you don't have to play squash, climb a mountain or do a triathlon.

Movement is possible without the latest sportswear or special equipment. All you need to do is to get slightly out of breath. Start with a goal of keeping it up for three minutes, then extend it to suit your schedule. Research shows that short sharp bursts of exercise are just as beneficial as long stretches. When you are having fun 'moving' it doesn't feel like exercise.

EXERCISE: Exercise and Movement

The object of this exercise is to get you moving.

- It could be a game of rugby, a kick around with the kids in the park, doing a bit more vigorous housework or walking up and down the stairs – whatever you choose, make it attainable. Change the activity every day if you wish – it doesn't matter.
- Commit to doing your movement or exercise every day. Start by getting out of breath and keeping it up for three minutes.
- Add a minute or two each day, ideally up to about 20 minutes, but it's better to do a little than none at all.

Enjoy it. Make it part of your daily routine.

Make Like a Tree (and Leave)

If you haven't found the movement you enjoy, why not try *zhan shuang*, which means 'stand like a tree' (but I couldn't resist the *Back to the Future* joke). It is a form of tai chi, a powerful way of channelling chi energy, the fundamental energy of life. It helps to dissipate the energy in your head from current worries. Try googling it to find out more.

Using a Thought Journal

Your thought journal should be getting full by now. Keep using it for your TEA Cycle assessments, and for jotting down what is happening to you on a day-to-day basis. Writing is a powerful way of getting things off your chest when there is no one to share your thoughts with. It also helps you to have a more objective view of events, and helps you to self-reflect about how you could have done things differently. It teaches you how to reframe thoughts and be more flexible and compassionate towards yourself and others.

Remember to date your entries, and do write them when the original thoughts, emotions and actions are fresh in your mind. Memory has a way of reconfiguring our view of what happened, biased by our own prejudices. Have you ever discussed an event in the past with a friend who was also there? How does your account of what you remember differ from theirs? It is quite possible that they remember things in a completely different way, and specific things that you thought were important are not in their retelling of the event.

EXERCISE: Testing Your Memory

This exercise can highlight the individual twist we put on memory.

- Without looking at your notes, choose an incident that you know you have written about in your notebook.
- Repeat the first phase of the TEA Cycle and write down what you remember of the event, how you felt and what you did.
- Compare it with your first entry. Did you leave anything out or embellish anything?

Ask yourself what impact that had.

Using a Gratitude Journal

Use your notebook or start another journal to use for your thoughts of gratitude. At the beginning or end of each day, write down one thing you are grateful for that day. They don't have to be gigantic events, they can be as general as gratitude for a roof over your head or a warm bed to sleep in, as exciting as buying a wedding dress, as specific as a good conversation with a friend, or as insignificant as the cinnamon swirl you picked up with your coffee. When you want to boost your mood, you can look back at them and notice how they affect you on an emotional and spiritual level.

EXERCISE: Your Gratitude Journal

Writing things down, rather than just thinking or saying them, makes them more powerful.

- Choose one thing every day and write it in your journal or notebook.
- Make some time to think about why you are grateful and how it makes you feel.

You will find that even the smallest things can have a big impact on making you feel better. Look at the journal entries to lift your spirits when you need to.

Talk About It

Talking about our problems with someone who is sympathetic is a good way of processing what has happened and finding a new perspective. You are not looking for someone who will be too antagonistic in their attitude because that might trigger your stress response in itself. However, having your negative attitudes challenged can make you think harder about your behaviour and how you can change onto a more positive track.

Talking therapy is a well-recognized way of dealing with problems of stress, so you may want to consider looking for some professional help. A group session might also help you. Discussing a problem with someone who really knows how you feel can be very beneficial.

EXERCISE: Conversation

Talk, talk, talk – but remember this is your problem and the last thing you want to do is lose the support of a good friend. Setting a time limit on the conversation might be a good idea – or call on Zoom as it will cut off after 40 minutes.

- Choose a friend or relative who is aware that you are having some problems with stress.
- Tell them you would like to discuss a sensitive incident.
- Keep the discussion going as long as it is helpful, but make sure you are coming away with the positives this person can bring not more negatives.

People often say they feel unburdened after a good conversation where they felt heard.

Emotional intelligence techniques are important when discussing issues around stress. It is not dissimilar to the TEA Cycle and is useful when working on your self-assessment questions. The steps are: describe the situation with specific details. Describe the associated behaviour and its impact. Observe and listen before giving empathetic feedback.

Don't be afraid of talking to yourself in a mirror. Many people find this really hard, but try giving yourself a compliment. It can help you to be more self-objective and self accepting.

Being Complimentary

We all appreciate a bit of praise or a compliment – well, at least I do. But sometimes we have to wait for someone to drop nuggets of happiness into our laps. Take control and learn to give them to yourself. I know it's hard to say good things about ourselves, but it's not boasting or showing off. Here are two ways to start identifying your strengths and being proud enough to shout about them (even if it is only to yourself at the beginning).

Try some mirror work. Louise Hay, motivational author of *You Can Heal Your Life,* used the concept of mirror work to help us become accustomed to saying good things about ourselves. Start slowly, but take a daily look at yourself in the mirror and say, 'I'm OK' or 'I love you' or anything nice that gets you out of the 'I hate me' blocks. This exercise sounds deceptively simple, but I challenge you to try it and then build up to looking at yourself for longer periods of time and saying nice things. You can journal about thoughts that come up.

EXERCISE: Mirror Work

This concept from Louise Hay is a great way of boosting your self-esteem and countering the negative impact of stress.

- Sit in front of a mirror and talk to yourself as though you were someone else.
- Pay yourself a compliment, such as 'that's a nice jumper'.
- Practise responding to that compliment. Don't reject it (oh, this old thing?!) acknowledge it with gratitude – 'Thank you. I like this one, too.'

You need to believe in a compliment for it to have the right impact, so be sincere. It will boost your self-esteem and self-confidence.

Boost Your Self-Esteem

Self-esteem is simply the way we see ourselves or the way we'd describe who we are to others. Imagine holding up a mirror, staring at yourself and logging all the characteristics you can see. It's tricky! We tend to do a character assassination, and home in on our weaknesses and the things we don't like about ourselves. We also spend too much time comparing ourselves to others. I would encourage you to focus on the positive attributes and measure all the good stuff about yourself. You are valuable, and you need to remind yourself of that.

EXERCISE: Define Your Talents

Another way to emphasise the good things about yourself is to ask friends or family to define what they think are your talents and strengths.

- What do you like about me emotionally or mentally?
- What do you like about the way I behave?
- What activities am I good at?
- What do you like about my physical characteristics?
- Do I have any special talents?

Use the answers to give yourself a pat on the back to build your self-esteem, giving you more strength to deal with stressful situations. Keep a note of these where you can easily find them and refer back to lift your spirits.

EXERCISE: Take Three Outside Appraisals

Keep boosting your self-esteem to help you avoid negative thought patterns that can both cause and be the result of stress.

- Ask three people who know you well, and who you trust, to answer the bullet-list questions in the exercise opposite about you, or frame your own questions.
- Write the short answers in your notebook, on paper or an index card and look at them regularly to boost your confidence and self-esteem.

Remembering your positive qualities during tough situations activates your courage and motivation; it's a great resource to have in your back pocket.

Challenge Your Core Beliefs

Some beliefs have been drilled into us since childhood; they are buried in our subconscious programmes and affect our behaviour in real time, making us repeat the same patterns of behaviour despite our best efforts?

Negative beliefs are the hardest to break. The first way to attack them is to make sure you do not mistake the general for the specific. You are not stupid but sometimes you do stupid things, so don't brutally hang on to the 'I am stupid' mantra. Be honest but kind: 'It was a stupid thing to do... but my motives were good.'

Look for evidence to understand why you behaved that way in those circumstances and to provide a more balanced assessment of your general behaviour. How often have you been stupid as opposed to how many times you have been sensible? Think through other possible ways of handling the situation. Forgive yourself for being stupid on one occasion, and don't extrapolate from one instance that you are stupid all of the time.

EXERCISE: Core Beliefs

Challenge the negative assumptions you make about yourself. Interrogate the idea that you are stupid, insensitive, unkind or any other quality. They cannot be 100% true all of the time.

- Choose a quality in yourself that you accept as partly true but deserves to be challenged.
- Choose an incident that demonstrates you showing that characteristic. Acknowledge why it didn't show you at your best by writing, 'I was stupid on that occasion because of ...'
- How would you behave given the same circumstances again?

This is designed to help you practice self-compassion, forgive yourself, and not to beat yourself up.

Acknowledge What Is Out of Your Control

Imagine a series of concentric circles. You are in a small circle in the middle and you have control of that circle. The next circle contains your close family and friends; you have some influence there but cannot enforce change. The next circle outward could be your work colleagues, then your neighbours, your bosses, and so on until you reach the national political situation and, beyond that, the world. As you step outside the boundary of your circle and beyond, notice how your ability to influence the behaviour or circumstances of others decreases.

When you feel out of control, ask yourself if you are placing too much focus and energy in the wrong place. Can you influence the outer circles directly or is that impossible? Is it better to operate within the boundaries of what you can personally affect? This will minimize the stress you feel from external factors that you cannot control – like getting irritated by people not doing what you ask – and prevent your threat response being triggered.

EXERCISE: Control and Power

This is just a fun way of demonstrating how far our control can stretch.

- Stand in the middle of a room and clear as much space as you can or, better still, go outdoors.

- Imagine you are in the middle of a circle with a metre (3-foot) radius, surrounded by 10 further concentric circles each a metre (3 feet) away from one another
- Have someone place a dozen items of various sizes and shapes further and further away from you within the circles – perhaps a book, a coin, a small stool, an apple, a saucepan and a cushion. It doesn't really matter what they are.
- First, pick up the items in the circle you are standing in. How long does it take you to collect up all the items? Possibly only a few seconds because you have control in your circle.
- Next, pick up the items in the second outer circle. Continue with the items in the third, fourth and fifth outer circles. At some point you will get tired, bored or annoyed that they are out of reach.

The lesson? Admit the limits of your personal power and ability to influence others.

There are some things that are not going to change, however much you may want them to, so we need to accept the situation and stop wasting valuable energy that can be better spent on practising positivity. But if you really want to make a difference, start planning the steps you will need to take to achieve that.

Reinhold Niebuhr's *Serenity Prayer*[16] is one of my favourite poems to repeat during difficult moments (substitute 'God' however you wish).

'God grant me the serenity to accept the things I cannot change, courage to change the things I can, and wisdom to know the difference.'

Build Your Confidence and Resilience

Confidence is faith and belief in your ability to achieve a goal. You get a buzz from seeing the results of your efforts. Confidence is not a fixed state, it goes up and it goes down. Tackling new activities or just pushing your abilities that little bit further can be a real confidence boost as it encourages you to step outside your comfort zone. It sets up a positive cycle of more confidence breeding greater competence. It brings a sense of happiness, security and safety, all the feelings that calm our nervous system and stop the stress response from firing.

Confidence is active – it generates more competence and skill. Don't be shy in praising yourself; the more you pat yourself on the back for doing a job well, the more your self-belief grows. Learning a new skill and succeeding bring more pleasure than repeating the same old things that you can do standing on your head. Stretch yourself! Your dopamine hormones will encourage you to repeat the things that feel good and are rewarding.

Thinking outside the box helps you expand skills, feel alive
and build your resilience muscles.

What exactly does resilience mean? It is the ability to withstand
and to recover from difficult conditions. Resilience can also
involve an element of growth, and expanding beyond your
existing comfort zone. Learning to cope with the unknown,
assessing situations quickly, learning and storing the experience
are crucial to becoming more resilient. If life was predictable
and pretty much the same string of events happened every day,
the word resilient would become obsolete, because there'd be
no fires to put out and no super-villains to fight.

Being resilient doesn't mean you will stop feeling scared
in the face of a problem – it means you will find the courage,
focus, speed and alertness to keep powering through
situations until you get the result you want. Plus you will
give yourself the essential space afterwards to recharge and
consolidate the new lessons learned. This is what you need to
think about when filling in your TEA Cycle events. Gradually,
you will become more able to predict emotions from thoughts
and actions from emotions.

Build up your resilience by trying new things!
Encountering new situations is a good thing. Okay, it might
be nerve-wracking at the time, but by now you are getting
really good at harnessing your energy and turning it to
challenge energy. Dealing with new experiences will stretch
your comfort zone, teaching you new tools and strategies.
Trust that, as uncomfortable as the situation might feel in

the moment, your response provides valuable information for the future.

Adding novelty to your life will open doors and broaden your horizons – and prevent boredom.

EXERCISE: Trying New Things

Push the boundaries of your comfort zone.

- Write a list of six new doable activities that you can action right away.
- Roll a dice and whichever number comes up, you must do the activity that day or that week.
- Allow yourself to feel the anxiety of not knowing which activity will come up, and the fear that you'll mess it up. Push past this, and keep your promise to yourself.

Keep it simple. By round two you'll have realised that you can learn new things, that uncertainty is a fact of life and you can deal with it, that anxiety levels go up and come down – and that's all okay. Oh yes, and if it all goes terribly wrong – what does it matter? Ask yourself, will this situation matter to me in a week's time, a month's time, or a year?

Recovering from Traumatic Stress

Researchers have observed humans handling distressing situations or enduring unspeakable atrocities or personal tragedies, and that many are able to get their lives back on track afterwards. Being stressed, even in the most severe of circumstances, doesn't necessarily break us; it can stretch us and help us develop resilience and coping strategies. Any of the strategies discussed in this chapter may be appropriate, alongside a professional therapist. As we grapple with ways to process grief, loss or change and make sense of it, we gradually make peace with the situation, which in turn reduces our suffering and makes us more appreciative of the good things in our lives.

Avoid Comparisons

Are you comparing your appearance and body shape to someone else's, or the position a colleague holds within a company or their salary? Are you observing how someone else's partner treats them compared to how your partner treats you? Deciding you are better than someone might sound like the best way to fast-track your self-esteem. However it can breed conceit, arrogance and unkindness. Deciding you are worse off than someone breeds self-hatred, self-pity and can generate a desire to self-harm. It's a loser's game either way.

The best advice to build genuine self-esteem is to stay in your own lane. When I came across this idea it made me feel a lot better about myself. Staying in your own lane means all you need to do is compete against yourself. You only need to compare the version of yourself today with the version of yourself yesterday. This way, positive incremental changes are totally unique. No more fear of missing out on anything.

Self-esteem is something that you build and maintain. Your perception of who you are changes with more self-knowledge and life experiences. Your self-perception changes in the light of new challenges. The truth is, even the most confident person can experience low esteem. But be wary of holding a negative view of yourself for a long period of time. Losing sight of how amazing you are can lead to depression and darker thoughts. If this ever happens to you, consult a friend or a health practitioner, they can give you a better understanding of the ways to get out of the rut.

EXERCISE: The Penny Jar

This is another way of boosting your self-esteem to help you steer clear of succumbing to the stress response.

- Find an empty jar.
- Every time you spot something you like about yourself, even if you repeat the same attribute from the day before, add a coin to the jar.
- As the jar fills, watch how it helps you place more value on yourself. It also acts as a visible reminder of your growing positive self image.

When the jar is full, spend it on a treat for yourself or a friend, or donate it to charity.

Time Management

Stress is often related to simply having too much to do. We try to keep all the plates spinning but if we lose concentration for a moment, wait for the inevitable crash! When you are working as hard as you can, you can't change your performance levels, therefore you have to do something about the amount of work. The key to this is that not everything is urgent. It may feel as though everything should be finished yesterday, but that is simply not possible. Learning to accurately assess your workload and stay calm takes practice, but is essential if you're going to avoid unnecessary stress.

Lists can be a procrastination tactic; you stop to write a list to avoid getting on with what you're supposed to be doing. However, in this instance they are an essential tool to help you sequence tasks. Write down each task that you have to do. Against each one give it a level of priority, for example, instant, urgent, moderately urgent, not urgent. Next, against each one write down how long the task will take. Allocate your agenda, working on the most urgent things first. If you prefer to get warmed up and gain some momentum and motivation, then do one or two easier tasks first. Finally, just do it!

Another option is complete disclosure, being honest about your priority list, and not keeping quiet until it is too late. Show your priority list to your boss and explain what you are doing to get everything done. If you could meet those deadlines by getting additional help, then ask for it.

EXERCISE: How to Prioritize

Learn to minimize stress by prioritizing your work.

- Ask yourself if the situation is really a problem. Could some of the work be delivered later?
- Are you lumping too many problems in one basket? Can you untangle them and separate them out?
- Grade them according to urgency.
- Ask for support, if you need it, or explain your planning.
- Decide which task you'll tackle first.

You will find that even going through the process reduces your stress levels. It's the difference between having a plan, and having no plan.

Maintaining All Your Positive Gains

When we feel better, we stop taking the 'medicine'. Our brain can conveniently forget how difficult things were a short while back. Being on a healthy eating plan to maintain your figure requires continuous monitoring of your diet. Likewise, maintaining your psychological and emotional health requires a similar discipline. Watch your intake of mind-bloating negative thoughts. Keep practising the exercises and strategies that work for you. We are all different, and as Forrest Gump said in the 1994 film of the same title: 'Life is like a box of chocolates. You never know what you're gonna get', so be prepared to try some of the ideas and see how it goes.

Stress Energy Assessment

Now you have read this chapter, rerun your Stress Energy Assessments (pages 14–15), applying your new understanding, and fill in your progress graph. You should, by now, be showing considerable improvement.

7

CULTIVATING A POSITIVE MINDSET

In the previous chapter we looked at specific strategies that will help us combat our negative stress responses and use our stress energy in more productive ways. In this chapter, we are going to look at how we can build a more resilient mindset going forwards to be able to handle things that potentially stress us out. It focuses on preventive measures and life skills that will help us to become more resilient, so that when faced with one of our stressors, we no longer experience extreme stress reactions.

Where we focus our attention will be essential to reducing stress.

What Is Your Dream?

Let's start thinking big. What are your life ambitions? Your dreams? Where do you want to be in three years, in ten years? We often put off making conscious choices and decisions about our lives in the long term. We use the excuse of the everyday things to keep us stuck in the present. Concentrating on the small things can stop us from reflecting on, where we are and where we want to go. Where we focus our attention is essential to changing our lives for the better and reducing stress.

EXERCISE: Maintaining Your Focus

Do you have a major ambition? Something that you really want to do with your life? Define it and keep it at the forefront of your plans.

- What is it you want (or don't want) out of life? Your dream. Your ambition. Write it down. It doesn't have to stay the same, but say what it is now.
- Clock in every week or so and record what you have done to advance toward your goal.
- Fire up desire, stay motivated and be the best you can be, following the adage: 'Where your attention goes, your energy will flow'.
- Stick post-it notes or sheets of paper around as a reminder to keep your eyes on the prize.

Never be afraid to change your goals. Know when to pivot.

Live in the Now

Are you fully present at the task in hand, or with the person you are talking to? I know this sounds like a strange thing to ask, but staying conscious of what's happening in the present moment can be really hard! We spend a lot of time living mentally and emotionally in the future or in the past. Why is it so difficult to live in the moment, right here, right now?

Humans are designed to be able to exercise predictive thinking – it's a valuable skill. But if you are thinking about all the things on your to-do list when a friend is talking to you about a problem they are having, neither of you is going to benefit much from the conversation. When you are future-gazing, you cannot be fully aware of the beauty of a bird that flits on to the hedge beside you. If you have your ear pressed against your phone, you'll miss the opportunity to chat to someone at the bus stop.

EXERCISE: Learning to Look

We are so often distracted by other sensual stimuli or thoughts and feelings that we forget to concentrate on one thing. Our brain enjoys the break from multi-tasking.

- Choose a photograph or picture that you really like and that has lots of detail – anything from an Old Master to a jigsaw puzzle. If you can't think of one, Google *The Great Piece of Turf* by Albrecht Dürer.
- Just look at it for five minutes. Do nothing else. Don't be distracted by a shopping list, background music, a cup of coffee.
- Become totally immersed in the detail.

You'll find that you see so much more than if you just glance at things. Try to bring this skill into your life. Sharpening your focus and concentration is a practice and an art.

The GROW Model

The art of goal setting and making things happen is a skill used by entrepreneurs, but you can copy it to apply to anything from a major project to doing the housework.

To achieve a big idea, you must have a dream, then break it down into steps and create a realistic schedule. The planning stages may feel uncomfortable, but recognize that as challenge energy because you know there's no need for threat energy, even though this may be a scary new adventure.

G = establish your GOALS: A series of small goals work best to get the work done, with an overarching mission goal to drive your motivation; be prepared to be flexible about your end goal.

Think about what you want to achieve and set boundaries. Open-ended tasks are less likely to be completed.

Set a schedule to drive progress. Time is something the brain understands. If the task is open-ended it will never get started or completed. The brain loves clear, concise instructions.

R = keep it REAL: Reality is preferable to fantasy and high expectations that never get fulfilled. Keep your feet on the ground.

O = look at all OPTIONS: Allow your creative ideas to flow. There are no wrong answers. How could you achieve your goal? What resources do you need? Does it involve anyone else?

W = WILL you do it?: Are you still excited by the plan unfolding? Rate your desire to do it on a scale of one to ten. If it's not a ten, ask yourself why.

Finally: Once the task is completed, reward yourself verbally or give yourself a small gift. Acknowledge internally this is a 'mission accomplished'. This part is critical to encourage the brain to give you dopamine, the reward hormone. It will encourage you to do similar activities again and start building new stronger neural networks in your brain to help you.

EXERCISE: The GROW model

This is a business model for project development that you can use for any aspect of your life; adapt it to suit something you want to achieve.

- Establish your main goal and a series of goals leading up to it.
- Set a schedule.
- Make a realistic plan.
- Examine the creative options.
- Make a decision, then go for it.

Learning Assertiveness – How to Say 'No'

To be assertive does not mean being aggressive or condescending. It is valuing yourself as being equal to everybody else and considering your own needs as well as theirs. Not being assertive can contribute to triggering your stress response or make a triggered response worse. There are only so many times you can be overlooked for a promotion, or your friends make you the designated driver on a night out, or your family lets you down. When you are crystal clear about what you want, you'll feel in control, calmer and gain some self-respect.

There's a saying, 'Knowing what you stand for stops you falling for everything'.

If someone asks you to do something, think about whether you really want to, or can, do it. If not, say no, and explain your reasons, if you like. Saying 'No' more often will keep you sane, stops you from being overburdened and creates room for inviting into your life the things that you do want.

Positivity and Realism

Accepting the truth of a situation does not mean you are resigned to nothing ever changing. It means that you accept what you can and cannot change, without amplifying or exaggerating the situation. It will help you keep a positive mental attitude and be grateful for the good things you have.

EXERCISE: Finding Solutions

A great Buddhist question to ask yourself when weighing up a decision is 'does this attitude push me towards a solution, or does it force me to shut down or lash out at others?'

- Think about a circumstance about which you have to make a decision.

Ask the question and decide which way you are directed.

Work Out What Is Important

Knowing the parts of your life that really matter to you is important. Things that may be significant to you may include: family, friends, children, romantic life, work, money, spirituality, health, personal growth and development, me-time, training and academic studies, holidays, home or the environment.

EXERCISE: Life Challenge Wheel

Investigate the areas of your life that are most important to you. If you lay them out inside a circle each life area is the spoke of a wheel. Here's a couple to think about: romance, home environment, me-time, hobbies, health and fitness, family, friends, work, finances, spirituality, creativity, rest and relaxation.

- Think about the areas of your life and rate how you feel about them right this moment on a scale of 1 to 10 (where 10 feels great and 1 feels bad). Do not worry if the rating is low.
- Take each one in turn and question what small action you could do within the next seven days to move a low-rated area up a notch. It doesn't have to be dramatic action, it just needs to be do-able.

Aim for all areas to be rated 10 in a couple of weeks' time!

Do What Makes You Happy

Do you know what makes you happy? The quickest way to find this is to track the activities you do every day and notice how much achievement, closeness and connection to other people they bring or how much you enjoyed them. If you like acronyms, which I do, this one is ACE (Achievement, Closeness, Enjoyment).

EXERCISE: ACE Tracking Journal

- Start drawing up your ACE inventory.
- Pick an activity you do, it could be travelling to work, making a meal, sewing, reading, watching TV, going for a walk, playing video games, chatting to friends, playing a game of football, or anything else you enjoy.
- Rate its ACE value on scale of 1–10, where 10 is the highest and 1 is the lowest.
- How much of a sense of achievement or accomplishment did you feel? Did it involve other people, and how strong was the connection or closeness? How much personal pleasure or enjoyment did it bring you? You might be surprised that the simplest activities can reap the biggest rewards.
- Try it with other activities.

Working with Your Breathing

The way our mind thinks influences the reactions in our bodies and vice versa. The way we breathe changes when we sense danger. When it speeds up, it make us think there's a problem; but our breathing can also help us to return to a state of relaxation when it slows down and returns to normal. The in-breath primes the body for action, the out-breath tells it to relax.

When stressed, we breathe in short, sharp bursts to take in more oxygen and our heartbeat races to pump oxygenated blood around the body. A side-effect of this is we can feel giddy or hyperventilate because the balance between oxygen (in-breath) and carbon dioxide (out-breath) is out of kilter. We mistakenly focus on the in-breath when trying to stay calm but the focus should be on the out-breath. Have you noticed when you let out a huge sigh of relief that a wave of relaxation follows? The exhale is the body's neurological reset button; it turns off the fight-and-flight reflex.

Try the breathing exercise below and use it regularly. If you are breathing correctly, it prevents the shallow breathing we've become accustomed to, which make the shoulders move up and down and prevents the lungs completely filling with oxygen. Remember, the brain needs oxygen to function well.

EXERCISE: Calm Your Breath

Try lying down and practising this with your hand placed on your stomach. If you do it correctly, your tummy will rise on the in-breath and fall on the out-breath.

- When you feel overwhelmed, maintain an even regular breath to break the erratic pattern you're stuck in.
- Make the exhale longer, breathing in for a count of three and out for six. Try to pause at the top of a breath and at the end of a breath – this makes your lungs work a bit harder.

To aid regulating your breath you could also try visualizing a regular pattern, such as rolling waves breaking onto the shore. Or visualize a shape (square, triangle, infinity loop) and say 'in' and 'out' as you follow the side of the shape in your mind or trace it out with you finger.

Relaxation

What do you imagine when I say the word 'relaxation'? Do you think about doing yoga in a quiet space, meditating for ten minutes to clear your mind, using progressive muscle relaxation (page 148), having a long hot bath or wandering through a quiet woodland? Any of those ideas are great to soothe your mind and calm your physiological reactions.

Just stopping and relaxing is something I confess to being bad at, but what suits me perfectly is choosing a calming activity that lets me hit the 'snooze' button on the busy side of life. Then I can pause, stand back, take a deep breath and slow down.

Whatever you choose, stop imposing other people's rules and make up your own. The only goal is to give your mind an opportunity to wind down, to quieten. I liken it to rocking a baby to sleep and saying soothing words such as 'you are safe, all is well, re-laaaax'.

PMR – Progressive Muscle Relaxation

On page 148 we looked at the system of tensing and releasing the muscles to relax and aid sleep. This is equally good as a relaxation technique any time of day, especially for people who find it hard to switch off.
By tensing then releasing muscle groups, it helps you recognize what a 'relaxed' muscle feels like, stops the flow of anxiety-inducing thoughts, and by the end of a sequence your body feels at ease.

Use Mantras and Affirmations

The spiritual followers of Hinduism or Buddhism improved their focus during meditation by repeating a mantra – a sound or a short word – which was sacred and created a sense of calm. Many people also use affirmations: short motivational phrases that sum up a situation. Here are a few examples.

- Anxiety isn't dangerous, it's just uncomfortable, but I can relax into it.
- I love myself for who I am.
- Today, I am bursting with energy and confidence.
- My mind achieves everything that I want.
- I have endless vitality and energy.
- Today I possess all the qualities needed for success.
- My mind loves learning, growing and expanding.

- I surround myself with supportive friends.
- I am courageous and I stand up for myself.
- My confidence grows stronger every day.

'I am safe, I am secure.' This is my favourite affirmation; it creates a sense of calm whenever I am flustered (along with regular slow breathing).

You can repeat affirmations to yourself or out loud to motivate and give you confidence and to trigger your body to produce the hormone serotonin that elevates mood.

Mantras and affirmations could be considered a form of self-hypnosis. You might not realize it, but you go in and out of light trance states throughout the day when your focus is intense. A trance is simply a narrow focus of attention, and if you get into a 'flow' state when doing a task it feels as though time stands still; you can also feel yourself jump out of a trance state when you leave a daydream.

EXERCISE: Affirmations

Think of a statement and make it your affirmation for the day.

- Keep your statement short sweet and memorable. One sentence is enough.

- Keep it based in the present moment, so you write 'I have xyz' or 'I am doing xyz', rather than 'I will do xyz' or 'I will be xyz' at some time in the future.
- Write it on a postcard or post-it note (something accessible).
- Look at the statement at least twice a day, and even more if you can.

Repetition is the way second-hand negative ideas were drilled into our heads during childhood, so why not deliberately create positive programming of your own choice as an adult.

Meditation and Mindfulness

Meditation is one step on from relaxation, when the body and mind are in harmony. You can try it on your own or choose a guided meditation where a teacher talks you through the various stages. There are countless methods, each one starting with breathing and relaxation. One method is to visualize yourself going slowly down a staircase one step at a time until you are at a deep level of relaxation. Remain there, letting your thoughts wander where they will, until you feel ready to gradually return to the real world.

When you focus on your heartbeat and breath at the same time, the mind drifts out of your head and into the body, pushing the overflow of thoughts about work, family, shopping or irritating neighbours to the back of your mind. Other ways of focusing include imagining a problem stepping backwards and shrinking, or imagining being able to turn the volume down on the internal chatter.

Mindfulness is essentially a state of being in the moment, totally immersed in whatever you are doing, non-judgemental and not reacting to stress triggers or other distractions. You can learn how to practise it through online apps or courses and it takes less practice than meditation. It can be achieved through focusing on ordinary everyday activities – washing the plates, brushing your teeth, going for a walk or riding through a park. When we learned to looked at a photo or painting on page 185, we were beginning our process of practising mindfulness.

EXERCISE: Mindfulness

Being fully in the moment suspends judgement and you see things as they really are.

- Use your five senses to notice what you see, hear, smell, taste or touch to bring your attention to the present moment.
- For example, if you were out walking and noticed a red flower, smelled a bonfire, felt the hard pavement under your foot or the sound of the traffic, you would repeat to yourself one word, such as – red (flower) – or smokey (bonfire) – or solid (pavement). You don't

deny what's happening via your senses, but nor do you paint a drama or story.

- Allow your mind to acknowledge the item but not to tell itself a long distracting story, which encourages it to hop around. Notice the detail of the item, relating it to all your senses.

When you slacken your focus, you should feel refreshed and energized.

Embrace any of the relaxation, mindfulness, meditation or breathing techniques at any time of the day. Whether it's for two minutes or 20 minutes. Every little intervention counts.

Change Requires Action

Unfulfilled hopes and dreams will create negative energy that brings you down; it is not part of a positive mindset.

You believe in climbing the promotional ladder, but your work doesn't excite you. You long to be a great parent for your kids, but you work longs hours and don't form a bond with them. You worry about being physically unfit, but you won't exercise or go to the gym. Change requires action, and action requires you to summon willpower or motivation.

Willpower is all very well but it takes a lot to keep motivated – I don't know the statistics on how many new year's resolutions are kept against how many are broken but I could guess! 'Intention', on the other hand, can have a surprisingly positive effect on behaviour. It can help you choose what you want to achieve and, despite setbacks and failures, enable you to dust yourself off, get back on course and start again.

Firstly, keep your goal small and fix a timescale. 'In three months, I want to be able to walk up the stairs without getting breathless'. You can attack your goal in different ways, you can stop and start, but make sure you keep returning to it over and over without feeling bad or guilty.

Have you heard of the expression, 'if you're going to fail, then fail forwards'? Well that's what the word intention will do for you. Try and try again but keep moving forwards. Start creating deliberate, conscious, attainable goals, instead of accidental negative ones that leave you feeling stressed, disappointed and demoralised.

EXERCISE: Setting Realistic Goals

Life doesn't always go to plan. We can't control every area of our lives because they overlap with other people's territories. We can voice, visualize and write down dreams and ambitions.

- Don't be afraid to dream big. Write down your dreams in your notebook.
- The magical strategy is finding your big fat 'why'. Dig deep and work out why the goal you've set means so much to you. Work out whether and how you can make a difference to your life and to that of others.
- Break your dream down into steps – small, achievable goals. Write them down so you have a clear blueprint.
- You can even reverse engineer the steps, that is work backwards from your success point. Ask yourself as many times as is needed until you have a long list of mini action steps of 'what had to happen just before I reached this point?'
- Don't be afraid to change and adapt. Aim to fulfil the first goal, but be prepared to evaluate and reset it.

Progress can feel like watching a tortoise running a marathon, so you need to celebrate each mini win and let the results spur you on towards your main goal.

Nutrition and Diet

This is a huge topic and one that would fill more than one book in itself. This is a basic summary that barely scratches the surface but does give you some pointers on what to think about.

There are slimming diets and fad diets, sensible ones and crazy ones. Cut down to basics, the advice of the medical profession is that you should follow a balanced diet comprising about 33% mixed fruit and vegetables, 33% starchy carbohydrates, 20% protein, 10% dairy and 4% unsaturated fats. If you are aware of portion control, you shouldn't have to worry about calories, although the bottom line is that if you consume more calories than you burn, you'll put on excess weight.

Being overweight is not good if you are suffering from stress. It does not make it easy for your body to cope with the physical symptoms of stress, plus it is not good for your self-esteem. Added to that it may limit your exercise options, which could otherwise help with your stress symptoms.

Some foods can also make us more anxious. Caffeine is a stimulant (as is nicotine). Sugar and fats, along with certain food additives, can increase feelings of anxiety. Triggering the stress response can make you crave more junk food, setting up an unhealthy cycle.

Comfort eating can be a real problem if you are suffering from stress – sometimes only a bar of chocolate seems to take the edge off the negative feelings you are experiencing. It is important to find healthier alternatives.

If you find it hard to work out a healthy diet, a good place to start would be the British Heart Foundation's Eatwell guide,[17] which gives clear and detailed guidance on following a healthy diet. You may also consider visiting a nutritionist, who can give you specific advice.

World of Scientific Research

Doctors and academics are learning to be more open with their research. They are starting to share information with the public about new findings. I realize everything needs to be tested thoroughly to protect the public, but some things are too important to keep under your hat for several years. It would be good to read things that can help us now, written in down-to-earth language that we can all understand.

Many well-respected doctors, psychologists and neuroscientists are speaking openly about their research, their new philosophical beliefs and how they relate to their daily lives. They have been mixing holistic medicine with the medical models and integrating alternative therapies with functional medicine and their work in the lab and with clients.

All this must be a positive in fine-tuning our knowledge of stress and how to navigate it.

Stress Energy Assessment

Now you have read this chapter, rerun your Stress Energy Assessments (pages 14–15), applying your new understanding, and fill in your progress graph.

CONCLUSION

Now we come to the final analysis. You have hopefully arrived at a point where you feel confident in understanding your own stress triggers and how to reduce them, and how to deal with any subsequent symptoms. You will be moving forward with your life, energized by a positive attitude.

Everyone who has read this book will have progressed in their own way. If you have read and put the advice into practice, and done the exercises, you will have made progress. This will provide a springboard for continued improvement.

At the outset, you completed a baseline Stress Energy Assessment of the impact of stress on your life.

Complete the exercises on pages 14–15 for a final time. Compare the initial and final results. I am confident that you will see just how far you have come. The data will highlight where you can apply even more stress management skills and achieve a better lifestyle.

As long as you are moving forward, the pace doesn't matter. Take everything at the speed that suits you and don't put yourself under pressure.

A Timely Reminder

As I have been researching and writing this book, during 2020–21, we have been living through the Covid-19 pandemic. It hardly seems possible that in early 2020, we were blissfully unaware of what was in store and – despite some countries coping better than others – at the time of writing we are still reeling from the fallout and will be for many years to come.

It has been a time of tremendous fear and uncertainty; a time when we have needed all our strategies to reduce the triggers and deal with the symptoms of stress on every level. From key workers on the frontline under tremendous pressure to keep essential services going, to the elderly in care homes, to each of us isolated from friends and family. The common factor is that despite having to deal with the stresses of the situation in our own personal lives, there has been a united goal and a desire to pull together.

The stress was real! We all had our stress response button triggered. However, the fear was invisible. There were no tigers, lions or bears to fight off. The enemy was psychological, within the mind. The ways in which the 'stress' energy was reinvested was inspiring: challenges were met, and bonding and connections were made, which is a great reminder that humans are resilient and rise above the inevitable biological, love-it or hate-it, stress response... again and again.

Find Purpose and Meaning In Daily Life

Having purpose and meaning are important. And finding this day to day helps us tolerate distressing moments. Have you noticed that once you give yourself a valid reason for doing the things you do, that you cope a lot better? You are persistent, confident and you don't give up despite discomfort or pain. Don't underestimate the tremendous value and joy to be gained by bringing meaning and purpose to the table.

I believe you are stronger, resourceful, resilient and more capable than you could ever imagine! I believe that you can use that strength to navigate your way to a place where you can see stress as a challenge and not a threat and let it propel you to a better life. Bon voyage!

ACKNOWLEDGEMENTS

Thank you to all the great people who gave me the opportunity and confidence to write my first book. You provided the encouragement, wisdom and guidance that kept me going – Jo Lal, Beth Bishop and Wendy Hobson. Thank you to all the researchers, professors and neuro-specialists who have blown my mind with new concepts and cutting-edge research in the field of neuroscience – Dr Sonia Lupien, Andrew Huberman, Bruce Lipton, Daniel Amen, Amy Morrin, Kelly McGonigal and Alia Crum – thank you for opening my mind and allowing yourselves to be vulnerable in the face of negativity from the naysayers. The pursuit of truth is all there is, because without fresh thought there would be no progress or innovation. Seize the day. Be of value to the human race now... rather than later.

Thank you also to my supportive partner Dave, my sister Trisha, and my friends Kiren, Liza, Linda, Adele, Roger, Adrian and Savia.

ENDNOTES

1. UK Government, 2020. 'Health And Safety At Work Summary Statistics For Great Britain'. hse.gov.uk/statistics/dayslost.htm (accessed February 2021)

2. Knoblauch M, 2019. 'Why 'Glass Half-Full' People Live More Fulfilling Lives', *New York Post*. nypost.com/2019/05/31/why-glass-half-full-people-live-more-fulfilling-lives (accessed February 2021)

3. Kroeneke K, Spitzer RL, Williams JBW, 2001. 'The PHQ9 Validity Of A Brief Depression Severity Measure', *J Gen Intern Med* 16(9): 606–613
    Pfizer, 2010. '*Pfizer To Offer Free Public Access To Mental Health Assessment*'. www.Pfizer.com/news/press-release/press-release-detail/Pfizer to offer free public access to mental health assessment tools to improve diagnosis and patient care (accessed February 2021)
    Access the patient health questionnaire (PHQ) here: www.phqscreeners.com

4. Dictionary.com (accessed February 2021)

5. Harris Poll, 2020. 'Stress In America 2020 Survey Signals A Growing Mental Health Crisis', *American Psychological Association*. www.apa.org/news/press/releases/2020/10/stress-mental-health-crisis (accessed February 2021)

6. Porges S, 2009. 'The Polyvagal Theory: New Insights Into Adaptive Reactions Of The Autonomic Nervous System', *Cleve Clin J Med* 76(2): 86–90

7. Please consult a medical practitioner if you are having suicidal thoughts or self harming.

8. Porges S, 2009. 'The Polyvagal Theory: New Insights Into Adaptive Reactions Of The Autonomic Nervous System', *Cleve Clin J Med* 76(2): 86–90

    Porges S, 2011. *The Polyvagal Theory: Neurophysiological foundations of Emotions, Attachment, Communication, and Self-regulation*, Norton

    Porges S, 2017. *The Pocket Guide to the Polyvagal Theory: The Transformative Power of Feeling Safe*, Norton

    Porges S, Dana D, 2018. *Clinical Applications of the Polyvagal Theory: The Emergence of Polyvagal-Informed Therapies*, Norton

9. Seery MD, 2013. 'The Biopsychosocial Model of Challenge And Threat: Using The Heart To Measure The Mind', *Social and Personality Psychology Compass* 7(9): 637–653

10. Website For Centre For Studies On Human Stress. www.humanstress.ca (accessed February 2021)

11. McLeod, SA, 2020. 'Maslow's Hierarchy Of Needs', *Simply Psychology*. www.simplypsychology.org/maslow.html (accessed Feb 2021)

12. Holmes TH, Rahe RH, 1967. 'The Social Readjustment Rating Scale', *Journal of Psychometric Research* 11: 213–218

13. American Psychological Association, 2021. 'Stress in America 2021: Pandemic Stress One Year On'. www.apa.org/news/press/releases/stress (accessed April 2021)

14. Karimova H, 2021. 'The Emotion Wheel: What It Is And How To Use It', *Positive Psychology*. positivepsychology.com/emotion-wheel (accessed Feb 2021)

15. Bennadi D, 2014. 'Self Medication: A Current Challenge', *Basic Clin Pharm* 5(1): 19–23. ncbi.nlm.nih.gov/pmc/articles/PMC4012703 (accessed February 2021)

16. Neibuhr R, 1951. *Serenity Prayer*.

17. British Heart Foundation. 'The Eatwell guide'. bhf.org.uk/informationsupport/support/healthy-living/healthy-eating/healthy-eating-toolkit/eatwell-plate (accessed Feb 2021)

Additional Reference Sources

Algoe SB et al, 2017. 'Oxytocin and Social Bonds: The Role of Oxytocin in Perceptions of Romantic Partners' Bonding Behavior', *Psychol Sci* 28(12): 1763–1772

Amen D, 2013. *Unleash the Power of the Female Brain*, Piatkus

Amen D, 2013. *Healing ADD Revised Edition: The Breakthrough Program that Allows You to See and Heal the 7 Types of ADD*, Berkeley Publishing Group

Amen D, 2017. *Memory Rescue: Supercharge Your Brain, Reverse Memory Loss, and Remember What Matters Most*, Tynedale Momentum

Carabotti M et al, 2015. 'The Gut-Brain Axis: Interactions Between Enteric Microbiota, Central and Enteric Nervous Systems', *Ann Gastroenterol* 28(2): 203–209

Carhartt RL, Nutt DJ, 2017. 'Serotonin and brain function: a tale of two receptors', *J Psychopharmacol* 31(9): 1091–1120

Casarella J, 2020. 'How Does Stress Affect Binge Eating?' webmd.com/mental-health/eating-disorders/binge-eating-disrder/stress-binge-eating-disorder#1 (accessed April 2021)

Crum, AJ, Salovey P, Achor S, 2013. 'Rethinking stress: The role of mindsets in determining the stress response', *Journal of Personality and Social Psychology* 104(4): 716–733

Cuncic, A, 2021. 'Why Generation Z Is More Open To Talking About Their Mental Health'. verywellmind.com/ why-gen-z-is-more-open-to-talking-about-their-mental-health-5104730 (accessed April 2021)

Kabat-Zinn J, 2006. 'Mindfulness-Based Interventions in Context: Past, Present, and Future', *Clinical Psychology: Science and Practice* 10(2): 144–156

Lachance L, Ramsey D, 2015. 'Food, Mood, and Brain Health: Implications for the Modern Clinician', *Mo Med* 112(2): 111–115

McGonigal K, 2015. *The Upside of Stress*, Avery

Morrin A, 2015. *13 Things Mentally Strong People Don't Do*, Harper Thorson

Tocino-Smith J, 2020. 'What is Eustress And How Is It Different Than Stress'. positivepsychology.com/what-is-eustress (accessed Feb 2021)

Volkow, ND et al, 2015. 'The Dopamine Motive System: Implications for Drug and Food Addiction', *Mo Med* 112(2): 111–115

Yilmaz, M, Huberman A, 2019. 'Fear: Its All In Your Line Of Sight'. doi.org/10.1016/j.cub.2019.10.008

USEFUL RESOURCES

UK

- Anxiety UK: Helpline: 03444 775 774, www.anxietyuk.org.uk
- Heads Together: www.headstogether.org.uk
- Hub of Hope: hubofhope.co.uk
- Mental Health Foundation UK: www.mentalhealth.org.uk
- Mind UK: www.mind.org.uk
- Rethink Mental Illness: www.rethink.org
- Samaritans: www.samaritans.org, helpline: 116 123
- Scottish Association for Mental Health (SAMH) (Scotland): www.samh.org.uk
- Shout: www.giveusashout.org, text 85258
- Young Minds: www.youngminds.org.uk

Europe

- Mental Health Europe: www.mhe-sme.org
- Mental Health Ireland: www.mentalhealthireland.ie

USA

- Anxiety & Depression Association of America: adaa.org
- HelpGuide: www.helpguide.org
- Mentalhealth.gov: www.mentalhealth.gov
- Mental Health America: www.mhanational.org

- National Alliance on Mental Illness (NAMI): www.nami.org
- National Institute of Mental Health: www.nimh.nih.gov
- Very Well Mind: www.verywellmind.com

Canada

- Anxiety Canada: www.anxietycanada.com
- Canadian Mental Health Association: cmha.ca
- Crisis Service Canada: www.ementalhealth.ca

Australia and New Zealand

- Anxiety New Zealand Trust: www.anxiety.org.nz
- Beyond Blue: www.beyondblue.org.au
- Head to Health: headtohealth.gov.au
- Health Direct: www.healthdirect.gov.au
- Mental Health Australia: mhaustralia.org
- Mental Health Foundation of New Zealand:
  www.mentalhealth.org.nz
- SANE Australia: www.sane.org

TriggerHub.org is one of the most elite and scientifically proven forms of mental health intervention

Trigger Publishing is the leading independent mental health and wellbeing publisher in the UK and US. Clinical and scientific research conducted by assistant professor Dr Kristin Kosyluk and her highly acclaimed team in the Department of Mental Health Law & Policy at the University of South Florida (USF), as well as complementary research by her peers across the US, has independently verified the power of lived experience as a core component in achieving mental health prosperity. Specifically, the lived experiences contained within our bibliotherapeutic books are intrinsic elements in reducing stigma, making those with poor mental health feel less alone, providing the privacy they need to heal, ensuring they know the essential steps to kick-start their own journeys to recovery, and providing hope and inspiration when they need it most.

Delivered through TriggerHub, our unique online portal and accompanying smartphone app, we make our library of bibliotherapeutic titles and other vital resources accessible to individuals and organizations anywhere, at any time and with complete privacy, a crucial element of recovery. As such, TriggerHub is the primary recommendation across the UK and US for the delivery of lived experiences.

At Trigger Publishing and TriggerHub, we proudly lead the way in making the unseen become seen. We are dedicated to humanizing mental health, breaking stigma and challenging outdated societal values to create real action and impact. Find out more about our world-leading work with lived experience and bibliotherapy via triggerhub. org, or by joining us on:

🐦 @triggerhub_
🅕 @triggerhub.org
📷 @triggerhub_